16LIVES

EDWARD DALY

The 16LIVES Series

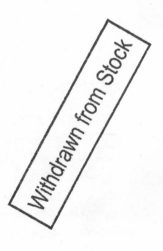

HELEN LITTON – AUTHOR OF 16LIVES: EDWARD DALY

Helen Litton, freelance indexer and editor, has written a series of illustrated histories and edited *Kathleen Clarke: Revolutionary Woman*, an autobiography (1991). Helen's paternal grandmother was Laura Daly O'Sullivan of Limerick, sister of Commandant Edward Daly and of Kathleen Daly, wife of Thomas Clarke.

LORCAN COLLINS – SERIES EDITOR

Lorcan Collins was born and raised in Dublin. A lifelong interest in Irish history led to the foundation of his hugely-popular 1916 Walking Tour in 1996. He co-authored *The Easter Rising : A Guide to Dublin in 1916* (O'Brien Press, 2000) with Conor Kostick. His biography of James Connolly was published in the *16 Lives* series in 2012. He is also a regular contributor to radio, television and historical journals. *16 Lives* is Lorcan's concept and he is co-editor of the series.

DR RUÁN O'DONNELL – SERIES EDITOR

Dr Ruán O'Donnell is a senior lecturer at the University of Limerick. A graduate of University College Dublin and the Australian National University, O'Donnell has published extensively on Irish Republicanism. Titles include *Robert Emmet and the Rising of 1803*, *The Impact of 1916* (editor), *Special Category, The IRA in English prisons 1968–1978* and *The O'Brien Pocket History of the Irish Famine*. He is a director of the Irish Manuscript Commission and a frequent contributor to the national and international media on the subject of Irish revolutionary history.

• •

16LIVES

EDWARD DALY

Helen Litton

THE O'BRIEN PRESS
DUBLIN

First published 2013 by
The O'Brien Press Ltd,
12 Terenure Road East, Rathgar,
Dublin 6, Ireland.
Tel: +353 1 4923333; Fax: +353 1 4922777
E-mail: books@obrien.ie
Website: www.obrien.ie
ISBN: 978-1-84717-272-3
Text © copyright Helen Litton 2013
Copyright for typesetting, layout, editing, design
© The O'Brien Press Ltd
Series concept: Lorcan Collins
British Library Cataloguing-in-Publication Data
A catalogue record for this title is available from the British Library
1 2 3 4 5 6 7 8
13 14 15 16 17
All quotations have been reproduced with original spelling and punctuation. Errors are author's own. Letters quoted in the appendices are in the care of the O'Sullivan family.

Printed and bound by CPI Group (UK) Ltd, Croydon, CR0 4YY
The paper used in this book is produced using pulp from managed forests.

PICTURE CREDITS

The author and publisher thank the following for permission to use photographs and illustrative material: front cover image: Courtesy of O'Sullivan family, Limerick; back cover: courtesy of Glucksman Library, University of Limerick; inside cover: National Library of Ireland; author photograph: courtesy of Edmund Ross Photography. Courtesy of O'Sullivan family, Limerick: section 1, p1 (bottom), p2 (top), p4 (bottom), p5 (bottom), p6 (top and bottom), p7 (top and bottom), p8 (bottom); section 2, p1, p7 (top and bottom), p8 (top and bottom). Courtesy of Glucksman Library, University of Limerick: section 1, p1 (top), p2 (bottom), p3 (top and bottom), p4 (top), p6 (top), p7 (both), p8 (top); section 2, p2. Courtesy of Helen Litton: section 1, p5 (top); Courtesy of Siobháin de hÓir: section 2, p6 (photographs by Frank Litton); Courtesy of National Library of Ireland: section 2, p3 (top), p4 (top KE108); Courtesy of Lorcan Collins: section 2, p3 (bottom), p4 (bottom), p5; Courtesy of Randel Hodkinson: section 1, p5 (bill head). If any involuntary infringement of copyright has ocurred, sincere apologies are offered and the owners of such copyright are requested to contact the publisher.

DEDICATION

To all descendants of the Daly family, Limerick

ACKNOWLEDGEMENTS

I hope this book will help to bring my grand-uncle Commandant Edward Daly out of relative obscurity, to a greater recognition of the part he played in the Easter Rising. I am very grateful to all at O'Brien Press for giving me this opportunity, particularly Michael O'Brien and my editor Susan Houlden; also series editors Lorcan Collins and Ruán O'Donnell: Lorcan was especially helpful.

I particularly wish to thank the following: Dr Anne Cameron, Archives Assistant, Andersonian Library, University of Strathclyde, Glasgow; Maira Canzonieri, Assistant Librarian, Royal College of Music, London; Linda Clayton, Association of Professional Genealogists in Ireland, for tracing Molly Keegan's life; Maeve Conlan, daughter of Johnny O'Connor, who gave me transcripts of interviews given by her father; Bernie Hannigan, daughter of Patrick Kelly, who gave me a copy of her father's memoir; Randel Hodkinson, Limerick; Lar Joye, National Museum of Ireland; Mary Monks, Vancouver; Paul O'Brien, for giving me a tour of the Four Courts battlefield; Professor Eunan O'Halpin, Trinity College, Dublin; Dr Terence O'Neill (Colonel, retd) for advice on military strategy; Joseph Scallan, Limerick, for tracking down archives; Deirdre Shortall, Dublin, for translating Irish texts.

I wish to thank the staff of the following institutions for their assistance: The Bureau of Military History, Cathal Brugha Barracks, Dublin; East Sussex Record Office, Lewes, East Sussex; The Frank McCourt Museum, Limerick; Ken Bergin and his staff, Glucksman Library, University of Limerick; Limerick City Archives; Limerick City Museum; Limerick County Museum; National Archives, Bishop Street, Dublin; National Archives, Kew, London; The National Library of Ireland; The National Museum of Ireland.

I thank my husband Frank for his unwavering love, support and patience, and all my family and friends for listening to my moans about 'lack of material'. Above all, my grateful thanks are due to Edward Daly's closest living relatives: his nephew and niece Edward and Laura Daly O'Sullivan of Limerick, his nieces Nóra and Mairéad de hÓir, also of Limerick, and their sister-in-law Siobháin de hÓir, of Dublin, who all gave generously of time, advice, anecdotes, photographs and documents. I must also thank my cousin Michael O'Nolan for help with documents and photographs, and all my relatives of the O'Nolan and O'Sullivan families. I happily dedicate this book to them, and to all the Daly descendants, however far-flung.

16LIVES Timeline

1845–51. The Great Hunger in Ireland. One million people die and over the next decades millions more emigrate.

1858, March 17. The Irish Republican Brotherhood, or Fenians, are formed with the express intention of overthrowing British rule in Ireland by whatever means necessary.

1867, February and March. Fenian Uprising.

1870, May. Home Rule movement founded by Isaac Butt, who had previously campaigned for amnesty for Fenian prisoners.

1879–81. The Land War. Violent agrarian agitation against English landlords.

1884, November 1. The Gaelic Athletic Association founded – immediately infiltrated by the Irish Republican Brotherhood (IRB).

1893, July 31. Gaelic League founded by Douglas Hyde and Eoin MacNeill. The *Gaelic Revival*, a period of Irish Nationalism, pride in the language, history, culture and sport.

1900, September. *Cumann na nGaedheal* (Irish Council) founded by Arthur Griffith.

1905–07. *Cumann na nGaedheal*, the Dungannon Clubs and the National Council are amalgamated to form *Sinn Féin* (We Ourselves).

1909, August. Countess Markievicz and Bulmer Hobson organise nationalist youths into *Na Fianna Éireann* (Warriors of Ireland) a kind of boy scout brigade.

1912, April. Asquith introduces the Third Home Rule Bill to the British Parliament. Passed by the Commons and rejected by the Lords, the Bill would have to become law due to the Parliament Act. Home Rule expected to be introduced for Ireland by autumn 1914.

1913, January. Sir Edward Carson and James Craig set up Ulster Volunteer Force (UVF) with the intention of defending Ulster against Home Rule.

1913. Jim Larkin, founder of the Irish Transport and General Workers' Union (ITGWU) calls for a workers' strike for better pay and conditions.

1913, August 31. Jim Larkin speaks at a banned rally on Sackville (O'Connell) Street; Bloody Sunday.

1913, November 23. James Connolly, Jack White and Jim Larkin establish the Irish Citizen Army (ICA) in order to protect strikers.

1913, November 25. The Irish Volunteers founded in Dublin to 'secure the rights and liberties common to all the people of Ireland'.

1914, March 20. Resignations of British officers force British government not to use British army to enforce Home Rule, an event known as the 'Curragh Mutiny'.

1914, April 2. In Dublin, Agnes O'Farrelly, Mary MacSwiney, Countess Markievicz and others establish Cumann na mBan as a women's volunteer force dedicated to establishing Irish freedom and assisting the Irish Volunteers.

1914, April 24. A shipment of 35,000 rifles and five million rounds of ammunition is landed at Larne for the UVF.

1914, July 26. Irish Volunteers unload a shipment of 900 rifles and 45,000 rounds of ammunition shipped from Germany aboard Erskine Childers' yacht, the *Asgard*. British troops fire on crowd on Bachelors Walk, Dublin. Three citizens are killed.

1914, August 4. Britain declares war on Germany. Home Rule for Ireland shelved for the duration of the First World War.

1914, September 9. Meeting held at Gaelic League headquarters between IRB and other extreme republicans. Initial decision made to stage an uprising while Britain is at war.

1914, September. 170,000 leave the Volunteers and form the National Volunteers or Redmondites. Only 11,000 remain as the Irish Volunteers under Eóin MacNeill.

1915, May–September. Military Council of the IRB is formed.

1915, August 1. Pearse gives fiery oration at the funeral of Jeremiah O'Donovan Rossa.

1916, January 19–22. James Connolly joins the IRB Military Council, thus ensuring that the ICA shall be involved in the Rising. Rising date confirmed for Easter.

1916, April 20, 4.15pm. *The Aud* arrives at Tralee Bay, laden with 20,000 German rifles for the Rising. Captain Karl Spindler waits in vain for a signal from shore.

1916, April 21, 2.15am. Roger Casement and his two companions go ashore from U–19 and land on Banna Strand. Casement is arrested at McKenna's Fort.

6.30pm. *The Aud* is captured by the British navy and forced to sail towards Cork Harbour.

22 April, 9.30am. *The Aud* is scuttled by her captain off Daunt's Rock.

10pm. Eóin MacNeill as chief-of-staff of the Irish Volunteers issues the countermanding order in Dublin to try to stop the Rising.

1916, April 23, 9am, Easter Sunday. The Military Council meets to discuss the situation, considering MacNeill has placed an advertisement in a Sunday newspaper halting all Volunteer operations. The Rising is put on hold for twenty-four hours. Hundreds of copies of *The Proclamation of the Republic* are printed in Liberty Hall.

1916, April 24, 12 noon, Easter Monday. The Rising begins in Dublin.

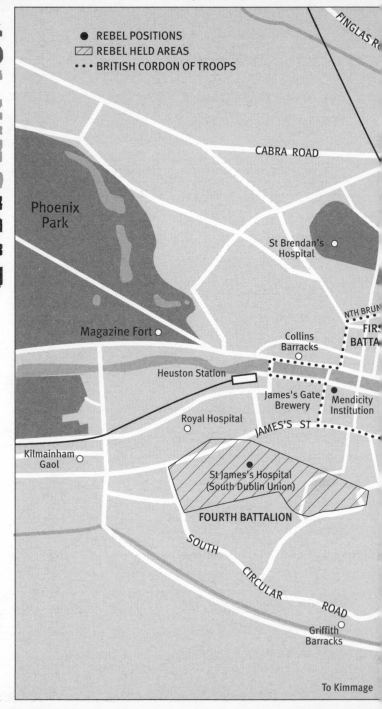

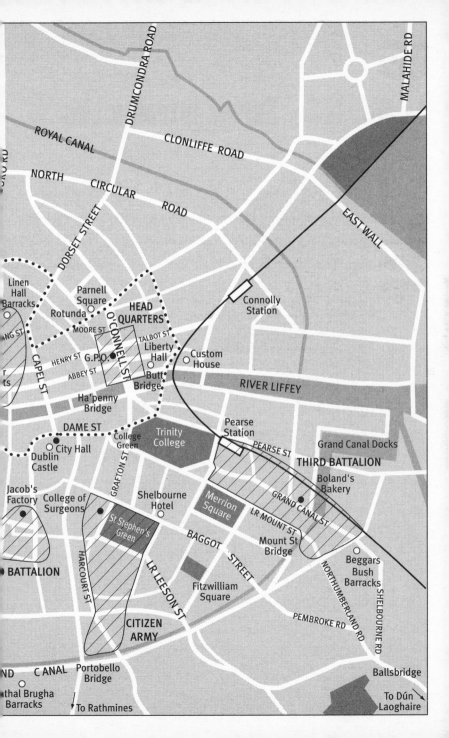

16LIVES – Series Introduction

This book is part of a series called *16 LIVES*, conceived with the objective of recording for posterity the lives of the sixteen men who were executed after the 1916 Easter Rising. Who were these people and what drove them to commit themselves to violent revolution?

The rank and file as well as the leadership were all from diverse backgrounds. Some were privileged and some had no material wealth. Some were highly educated writers, poets or teachers and others had little formal schooling. Their common desire, to set Ireland on the road to national freedom, united them under the one banner of the army of the Irish Republic. They occupied key buildings in Dublin and around Ireland for one week before they were forced to surrender. The leaders were singled out for harsh treatment and all sixteen men were executed for their role in the Rising.

Meticulously researched yet written in an accessible fashion, the *16 LIVES* biographies can be read as individual volumes but together they make a highly collectible series.

Lorcan Collins & Dr Ruán O'Donnell,
16 Lives *Series Editors*

CONTENTS

PROLOGUE

On 9 September 1890, the *Limerick Reporter and Tipperary Vindicator* reported sadly: 'The death of Mr Edward Daly ... which took place rather suddenly at his residence this day, is much regretted by his family and a large circle of friends.' He was buried on Thursday 11 September, in Mount St Lawrence cemetery, after one of the largest funerals ever seen in Limerick. The cortège was accompanied by several thousand mourners, as bands played funeral airs and men took turns in shouldering the coffin along the shuttered, silent main streets.

The late Edward Daly was undoubtedly a respected man in Limerick's nationalist circles, having at the age of seventeen spent time in prison for suspected participation in the Fenian movement, a physical-force republican organisation. His daughter Kathleen spoke of his funeral as 'the biggest spontaneous tribute to a man that I have ever seen'.[1] However, it is quite clear from the newspaper accounts that his funeral was deliberately used as the occasion for a massive nationalist protest against the imprisonment of his brother John.

The *Munster News* stated proudly:

Let no man libel or misrepresent the feelings of those four or five thousand mourners – there was not one amongst them who did not detest and condemn the crime with which John Daly stands charged, but ... they met and marched ... to show they believed with the dead man in his brother's innocence.[2]

The *Limerick Reporter* averred:

No matter how estimable was Mr Edward Daly in all the relations of life, his funeral procession, which a magnate might envy, was principally indebted in its most imposing features to the fact that it was the funeral of the brother of the persecuted, the high-souled and unpurchasable John Daly, English felon and Irish patriot.[3]

John Daly was living out his life sentence of penal servitude, for treason and dynamite offences, in Chatham Prison in Kent, which was notorious for its treatment of Fenian prisoners. The Limerick Amnesty Committee, led by his brother Edward, worked tirelessly for his release. Indeed, Edward's death at the age of forty-one, of heart disease, was partly blamed on the anxiety caused by his brother's situation, and the exhaustion of the amnesty campaign.

Although Edward Daly might not have been a nationalist icon, as his brother was, his legacy to Irish nationalism was none the less important. Five months after his death, his widow Catharine bore a son, John Edward (Ned) Daly, who was to commit his life to Ireland's cause at Easter, 1916.

Chapter One

1840s–1906

The Dalys of Limerick

Commandant Edward Daly was executed on 4 May 1916, aged twenty-five, having been court-martialled for rebellion. Born in Limerick, he was one of the youngest of those executed, and the youngest commandant in the Irish Volunteers. He was also the brother-in-law of Tom Clarke, the dedicated revolutionary who was one of the main movers of the Easter Rising. This biography tells of a lazy schoolboy, a bored office worker, an apparently vain and frivolous young man, who transformed himself into a brave and dedicated leader of the First Battalion of the Irish Volunteers.

His family background, of course, was the start of it. The Limerick family into which Ned Daly was born was reputedly descended from a 'scribe', John Daly, from County Galway, who may have been a member of the United Irishmen, the organisation responsible for the 1798 rebellion. The scribe's son, also John, lived at Harvey's Quay, Limerick, and worked as a foreman in James Harvey and Sons'Timber Yard. An excellent singer, this John was a moderate in politics. He supported Daniel O'Connell's Repeal movement, a non-violent pressure group seeking the repeal of the 1801 Act of Union. This Act had abolished Ireland's separate parliament, and brought Ireland fully under British control.

Two of the foreman's sons John (*b*1845) and Edward (*b*1848) espoused more radical politics, and in the 1860s they joined the Fenians, a republican group established in 1858 which advocated the use of physical force to win Ireland's freedom. It was an extremely secretive organisation; when John had sworn the oath, he was astonished to find that his younger brother Edward was already a member, along with every other young man he knew. Although their father believed in peaceful politics, their mother Margaret was more supportive of the Fenian cause, as was their sister Laura (known as Lollie).

In late 1866, the two brothers were arrested after an informer revealed their membership of the Fenians. The magistrate urged Edward not to be influenced by his brother, who was clearly bent on a course of crime. Edward 'answered him coolly by saying that if he had anything to say his brother would say it for him. How I longed,' wrote John later, 'for a chance to throw my arms around him,' but the handcuffs prevented him. Edward spent two weeks in

Limerick Jail. John was later released on bail, in time to take part in the failed Fenian rebellion of 1867, and subsequently made his way to the United States of America. Six years later, Edward married Catharine O'Mara of Ballingarry, County Limerick in January, 1873.[1] For a while the couple lived with his parents, and did not start a family until they had a home of their own. Eileen was born in 1876, the first of their eight daughters.[2] Edward worked as a lath-splitter, a skilled craft, at Spaight's Timber Yard in Limerick, during the 1870s. Between 1882 and 1884 he was an attendant at St George's Asylum, Burgess Hill, Sussex, but left that job on the arrest of his brother John.[3] He then seems to have worked as a clerk, possibly back in Spaight's. At the time of his death in 1890 he was a weighmaster for the Limerick Harbour Board, but had been in poor health for some time, suffering from a heart condition. When the LHB discussed his death at their next meeting, his job was referred to as a 'sinecure' (ie a position with little responsibility), and he was not replaced.[4]

Upon his death an article appeared in the *Munster News*, on 10 September 1890, emphasising the help he had been given:

> For some time it was thought that he would last a few years yet, owing to the extreme kindness with which he was treated during a stay in St John's Hospital, and the Harbour Board ... by giving him lengthened leave, showed their appreciation of his faithfulness to duty, but all was of no avail.

The newspaper urged sympathisers to provide for his family:

> By his early death he has left a large and helpless family almost totally unprovided for .... It is well known that the services of the Dalys have ever been given freely in the cause of fatherland.

It was indeed a large family, consisting of the widowed Catharine, her mother-in-law and sister-in-law, and her eight daughters: Eileen, Margaret (Madge), Kathleen, Agnes, Laura, Caroline (Carrie), Annie and Nora. The eldest of the girls was fourteen, and their mother was pregnant again.

A public meeting was held in the Town Hall on 17 September, and a sub-committee was established by nationalist councillors to collect subscriptions for the 'Edward Daly Family Sustentation Fund'.[5] It started with £5; by January it had reached around £130 (about £8,000 today). The amounts collected were published each week, and the collection continued until the following August. The final total reached is unclear, and subscriptions began falling away.

Edward's brother John, serving his penitential sentence in England, was not told at the time by the family about his brother's death, but he had known Edward was ill. Writing to his niece Eileen, in a letter published in the *Munster News* (11 March 1891), he said:

> Tell him, that I felt somewhat put out at his not writing to

me, but when I heard that he was or had been very sick, oh! Then my heart went out to him, and I could think of him only as the brother who had suffered with me, fought a good fight side by side with me and who would, I am sure, freely share my present sufferings if it were necessary.

John Edward Daly, always known as Ned or Eddie, was born on 25 February 1891 at 22 Frederick Street (now O'Curry Street), Limerick. The sudden death of their father six months earlier had ended the childhood of the three eldest girls, Eileen, Madge and Kathleen, as they took on heavy responsibilities. His mother was trying hard to cope with her new circumstances. Even though her last child was the longed-for son, she found it difficult to focus on him, as though it was all too much to bear. Her daughter Kathleen later wrote:

> She seemed resentful that there was no father to whom she could present this little son. Then, gradually, she became absorbed in him. He was very frail, and perhaps this drew her to him more than a robust child would have done ...

Two of his sisters walked five miles each day to a farm for milk which was guaranteed free of disease, and this level of anxious care would hover over his whole childhood.[6]

The Edward Daly Fund ultimately enabled the family to buy a public house in Shannon Street, and Mrs Daly put a hopeful advertisement in the *Munster News* (19 December 1891):

Mrs Edward Daly begs to announce to her numerous friends and the general public that she has just re-opened the Old Established Bar, No. 3 Shannon Street, where she hopes to be favoured with their patronage and support.

However, the family had no experience in running such a business, and it failed after a year or so. Nationalist sympathisers were very supportive in propping up the bar, but less active in paying off the 'slates' they had run up.

Mrs Daly and her sister-in-law Lollie had once run a thriving business as trained dressmakers, but the notoriety of John Daly's arrest for Fenian activities had driven many respectable clients away. For the next couple of years, the two ladies presumably worked as they could in this profession. The older girls may have worked as shop assistants or sold craftwork, at which Carrie in particular was skilled. Madge, the second eldest, regarded as the brightest of the family, stayed on longer at school, as a pupil-teacher. The girls all attended the Presentation Convent in Sexton Street; their mother washed their pinafores every night, so they could present a good appearance.

At this low point in the family fortunes, a saviour arrived from overseas. James and Michael Daly, older brothers of Edward and John, had emigrated to Australia, one in the 1850s and the other in 1862. They had settled in the French island colony of New Caledonia, and prospered there as traders and sheep-farmers. Now James, whose own children had reached adulthood, decided to take care of his late brother's family. (Michael, who married three times and is said to have run through three fortunes, never returned to Ireland.)[7]

Arriving in Limerick in 1894, James moved the whole family to 'Clonlong', a large two-storey house with extensive grounds on the Tipperary road. Two of his nieces became shop assistants in Cannock's department store, and he apprenticed Kathleen to a dressmaker. She was interested in a musical career, but he refused to provide lessons for her because, he said, the money he had spent on his own daughter's musical training had been thrown away.[8]

A photograph taken after James's arrival, in 1894, shows the large family circle in which Ned Daly spent his childhood. His mother Catharine stands to the left, next to James and his sister Lollie, with their mother Margaret (née Hayes) sitting in the middle. The daughters range in age from Eileen, aged twenty, to Nora, aged six. Ned, aged three, can be seen in front in a sailor suit, holding a toy rifle.

The heavily-bearded young man to the right is Jim Jones, who had been informally adopted by the Dalys at three months old when his father Michael died. The family was grateful to Michael Jones, a naval engineer, for helping to smuggle John Daly to the USA in 1867. Jim's mother (née Lahiff) emigrated to the USA when she was widowed, but never sent for her son as she had promised.

Young Jim, a tireless secretary of the Limerick Amnesty

campaign for Fenian prisoners, and a 'big brother' to the Daly children, sadly died soon after this photograph was taken, in July 1894, aged twenty-six. He may have died of cholera, which spreads through infected water supplies and kills very rapidly.[9] His death must have been a huge shock to them all, particularly Lollie Daly, who had treated him as her own child. Three-year-old Ned had lost the only man of the family, scarcely replaced by an elderly and unfamiliar 'Uncle James'. Jim Jones was buried in the Daly grave in Mount St Lawrence cemetery, Limerick.

ERIN'S WELCOME TO JOHN DALY

Come close to my bosom my patriot peerless
My brightest, my sturdiest, bravest and best,
So loving and faithful, so fervent and fearless,
My high-hearted hero, come close to my breast …

Come, JOHN, come as swift as the flash of a cannon
To your dear native city, the banks and the bowers
Of your dearly loved river, the far-flashing Shannon,
Where in childhood you wandered amid the wild flowers.

He comes, see he comes! Let your banners flaunt gaily,
He comes! Let the whole nation thrill with his praise.
Let melody welcome untameable DALY,
Let rockets ascend, and let tarbarrels blaze.[10]

In 1896, when Ned was five years old, this crowded household was enlarged by one. His uncle John, aged fifty-one, Convict No. K562, was released from Portland Prison, where he had been moved from Chatham in 1891.

Having escaped to the USA in 1867, John had joined Clan na Gael, the American Fenian movement, and continued to work for Irish independence. He was sent back to Ireland in 1876 to work with the Irish Republican Brotherhood (IRB), as the Irish Fenians were now known. He became an IRB Central Organiser, and worked for some time as an attendant at St George's Asylum, Burgess Hill, as his brother was also to do.[11] Clan na Gael began to plan a dynamiting campaign in Britain, and indeed later succeeded in 1885 in bombing Westminster and the Tower of London.[12] John Daly, returning from the USA apparently as part of this campaign, arrived in Birmingham in April 1884, and was immediately arrested for dynamite offences and sentenced to life imprisonment for treason.

It was believed by his supporters that he had been framed; a statement by the Birmingham chief constable seems to have admitted this, saying that explosives had been obtained in America by an Irish police confederate, and delivered to Daly.[13] However, a well-known 'spycatcher-general' was adamant that Daly had ordered the bombs himself, and intended to throw one of them from the Gallery of the House of Commons, sacrificing his own life if necessary.[14] John himself protested at his trial at Warwick Assizes, in July 1884, that he abhorred physical violence, but he admitted having buried a canister of nitroglycerine in the garden where he was staying.

A man of strong physique and imposing presence, and a gifted orator, John defended himself at his trial, and declared himself willing to endure any sacrifice for his country:

Why, what was love? Was it not a divine inspiration – an inspiration given to man by God? A man without the feeling of love was not fit to live, was not a proper member of the community, and he thanked his God that he at least had love … If he was sent to a dungeon because of that love for his country, would it cure the offence? No, his love would still remain.[15]

The Limerick branch of the Amnesty Association had worked tirelessly for his release. The Daly home in Clonlong was the centre of this activity, under Jim Jones, who was secretary; the girls sent out appeals and correspondence and arranged public meetings. Kathleen recalled:

I watched everything he [Jim] did, and felt very proud when he allowed me to put the stamps on the letters he was sending out. Later he allowed me to fold the circulars for the post – I am sure I plagued him with my pleading to be allowed to help. In my imagination I was helping to free Uncle John and, of course, Ireland.[16]

As a result of a long and high-profile campaign, John was elected MP for Limerick in 1893, while still a prisoner. He was disqualified as a felon, of course, but in any case would have boycotted the parliament.

The child Ned would have been too young to participate in all this, but he must have been affected by the frenetic comings and goings, and the tension whenever a letter arrived from the English prisons where Daly was held. Twice, in 1886 and 1888, Edward and Lollie had been called urgently to England because their brother was seriously ill, and expected to die. The crisis in 1886 caused Edward to miss the birth of his daughter Annie; in 1888 John was poisoned by belladonna, having apparently been given the wrong medicine in error. Fortunately, he recovered each time, and his brother and sister would return exhausted by the stressful boat and train journeys.

Conditions for Fenian prisoners were notoriously harsh, and included solitary confinement, poor diet, broken sleep and back-breaking work. Visits were few and strictly controlled, and correspondence was heavily censored. Prisoners were forbidden to touch or speak to one another, and the environment was one of severe sensory deprivation. Many of the prisoners went mad under this treatment. John Daly kept up what correspondence he could with his family, and his flowery oratorical style expressed itself in exhortations to his brother Edward:

Take them [the children] into the country all you can, let them be amongst the fields and the wild flowers. Let them see the land and all the beauties of it. Have them on the Shannon, glorious Shannon, home of my heart's love I will never see more …

Pour into their young minds all you know of our Country's history! teach them how to love everything that is beautiful in Nature – how to love truth and honour, and how to hate everything that is wrong, that is mean, that is tyrannical and oppressive …

You must not take from this that I wish your daughters to become politicians, or to take to stumping the Country and ornamenting the gaols. Oh no, God forbid that, but I would have them fit to be Mothers, Spartan Mothers or Limerick Mothers such as our City could once boast of.[17]

John Daly was finally released because he went on hunger-strike, and his health was severely threatened. He was given amnesty on 15 July 1896 as a 'ticket-of-leave' man, which meant that he was released 'under licence', with strict conditions of behaviour and travel. His brother James, meeting him at the prison gate, took him to Paris, where some of James's family were living, to regain his strength; they stayed at the Hotel de Florence.[18] The first thing that struck Daly on his release was the sound of women's voices – he had hardly heard a woman speak in twelve years, apart from the rare visits of his sister Lollie. Catching sight of himself in the railway station mirror, he was shocked at how old he looked. He was described as having a nervous and excitable manner, and appearing prematurely aged, unable to step out with confidence.[19]

Arriving in Dublin in September, he was greeted by a monster torchlight procession. In Limerick, his carriage was pulled by dozens of men through the streets, and the celebrations went on all night. The excitement when he went through the door to greet his mother was intense. John was now home to stay, a massively popular and heroic figure. He had no intention of abiding by his 'ticket-of-leave' conditions, and immediately began a series of propaganda lectures for the Amnesty Association all over Ireland, including Ulster, and in the larger British cities.

After four years as the family mainstay, James Daly decided that it was time for him to move on. It was apparently axiomatic in the family that two Daly men could not live for long in the same house, and the brothers had been quarrelling. James was a constitutional nationalist, and supported the Irish Parliamentary Party. The Fenian physical force tradition was anathema to him, and this created difficulties with his nieces' political views, as well as those of his brother. He left Limerick in March 1898, and died in December 1900 in New Mayo, Australia.

When James decided to leave, his money went too. John realised that he was now responsible for the support of his mother, his sister, his sister-in-law, and the younger members of the family, but he had no means of employment. In this extremity, and building on the great success of his lectures so far, he contacted his old comrade John Devoy, of Clan na Gael. A fundraising tour of the USA was organised, beginning in New York in November 1897.

This was a huge financial and propaganda success, visiting cities with large Irish populations such as Boston, Detroit, Philadelphia and Baltimore. John, a gifted and passionate speaker, won Irish-American hearts with his emotional accounts of prison life, and his pleas for the remaining prisoners to be set free. The charismatic young beauty Maud Gonne, who had captivated Limerick with her campaigning when John was put up for parliament, accompanied him. They were greeted everywhere with massive demonstrations and patriotic banquets.[20]

In May 1898, John Daly arrived back in Limerick, financially secure at last. He had enough capital to start a business, and decided to open a bakery. An old friend, a foreman baker, taught him the business, and he set up a shop at 26 William Street, with a bakery behind, and storage space for the four or five horse-drawn delivery vans. Apparently the vanmen would look after the horses themselves at night; one of them, asked where he kept his horse, said, 'Behind the piano.'

Several of his nieces worked in the shop, which also sold eggs, sweets and cakes, and they were paid a half-crown weekly (two shillings and six pence). Carrie specialised in confectionery. Kathleen, however, had a flourishing dress-making business by this time, and refused to work for her uncle.[21] Agnes opened the shop every morning, walking in from Clonlong with eggs from their mother's chickens. The family soon moved in from Clonlong, however, to the house in William Street.

The name *Seágan Ua Dálaig* (John Daly in Irish), painted over the shop doors and on the delivery vans, was a deliber-ate nationalist statement. On opening day, John hired a tra-ditional singer to chant his praises outside the shop, and gave out a free loaf to every customer. The business prospered, and by 1912 John was able to expand into Sarsfield Street, taking over Carmody's Bakery there and turning it into a confectioner's shop.

Limerick at the end of the nineteenth century was a thriv-ing port, exporting beef, oats and wheat to the USA and Britain and importing timber, coal and iron. It had a popu-lation of about 35,000, with a prosperous Protestant upper class and a growing Catholic middle class. It also had a very vigorous trade union movement. John Daly became a rally-ing point for Limerick nationalist politics, and fought hard to win a seat on the City Council, but efforts were made to disqualify him from standing, as he was a convicted felon.

He was blackballed when he attempted to join the Shannon Rowing Club. Immediately, Limerick's nationalist working population opened a subscription list towards a rowing-boat for him. This was presented with much ceremony on the banks of the Shannon, following a torchlight procession accompanied by marching bands. At the head of the procession was a wagon carrying the boat, from which floated the Irish and American flags; the wagon was drawn by four horses with an outrider in green livery. The boat was christened *Lua-Tagna* ('Swift to Avenge').[22]

Daly raised his profile even further through involvement in the 1898 centenary commemoration of the United Irishmen. In early summer he welcomed Maud Gonne to Castlebar, County Mayo, where a famous battle had taken place in 1798, and presented her with an old French coin and a bullet from the period.[23] He also spoke at pro-Boer meetings, which condemned Britain's actions in the Boer War (1899–1902).

His political career was fortunate in its timing. A massive extension to the franchise in 1884 meant that most male heads of households now had a vote, and artisans and labourers provided the bulk of his support. He headed the local election poll in 1899, and was swept into office as Limerick's first nationalist mayor. His first act was to order the removal of the Royal Arms from the front of Limerick City Hall. His link on the mayoral chain depicts two crossed pikes and a pair of handcuffs.

John Daly was mayor for three years, retiring in 1902, and

was made a Freeman of Limerick in 1904. He turned the first sod for Limerick's electrical supply in 1902, and is supposed to have been the first to suggest using the Shannon for electrical power – the idea was rejected as impractical. Interested in new technology, he was vilified by Limerick's horse cabbies and carters when he voted for the introduction of electric trams.[24] He presented the Freedom of Limerick to noted nationalists James F Egan (who had been tried and convicted with him in 1884) and Maud Gonne on 10 May 1900.[25]

This must all have been a most stimulating environment for any child – huge political meetings, torchlight processions, living in the home of Ireland's most prominent ex-political prisoner, a hub of passionate political activity. But in his early years, Ned did not seem to promise well. A family anecdote has this spoilt lad throwing stones at the unfortunate maid who was bringing him to school, because he was embarrassed at having to walk with a countrywoman wearing an old-fashioned shawl. This must have been while he was attending the Presentation Convent in Sexton Street, until he was seven. He moved to the Christian Brothers in Sexton Street in 1899.

His school records list him as 'John Edward Daly', his baptismal name; his residence is given as William Street, and his parent (or guardian) as 'shopkeeper'.[26] He made his First Holy Communion in St Michael's Church on 26 May 1901. He left school in 1906, aged fifteen, having shown no particular academic promise. A friend of the Dalys later asserted that John Daly despised the formal education system of the time, and refused to allow Ned to sit for the state examinations.[27] However, there is an Intermediate Education certificate (Junior Grade) for Ned, dated 1905, which lists passes in English literature and composition, arithmetic, algebra, French and science.

History does not figure on this list, but it was undoubtedly on the curriculum. The Christian Brothers were noted for their use of Irish history to inspire nationalism in their pupils. The introduction to their *Irish History Reader* states that pupils 'must be taught that Irishmen, claiming the right to make their own laws, should never rest content until their native Parliament is restored; and that Ireland looks to them, when grown to man's estate, to act the part of true men in furthering the sacred cause of nationhood'.[28]

If Ned needed any further encouragement in this direction, it was available in his home. His aunt Lollie Daly, whose maternal uncle had been a teacher, was a well-educated woman with a great memory.[29] She would keep the Daly children enthralled with her tales of Irish history, dwelling on glorious and romantic deeds, particularly in relation to the Fenians whom she had known in her youth. Kathleen later wrote:

Mother would say, 'Have you no better sense, Lollie, keeping the children from their beds with your rambling?' but the effect of that rambling in later years brought us through one of the most difficult periods of our history with our heads up; we knew our history.[30]

Tensions developed in the family circle as the younger children grew up. The old Fenian, despite being an atheistic revolutionary, set tough standards of discipline for his high-spirited nieces and nephew. These were frequently ignored, as Carrie and Laura, for example, used to climb out the windows to attend dances. Young Ned could be seen downtown in the evenings, making the most of Limerick's cultural life – concerts, theatres, silent films at the Abbey Kinema.

Home life was crowded and noisy, with the coming and going of numerous visitors, cut-throat card games, musical evenings – Kathleen played a mean piano, and Ned's singing was greatly admired – and invariably a number of dogs and cats. Summers were spent in Kilkee, County Clare, in the immemorial fashion of Limerick's middle classes. The Daly family rented one of the larger houses there, Kilkee Lodge, on the Strand Line.

In the Census of 1901, the Daly home at 26 Lower William Street is described as a 'first-class' house, with ten rooms, and eight windows in front (including the shopfront). However, the family does not figure in the Census of 1911, and John may have refused to co-operate with it as a nationalist protest; political tensions had heightened by then.

The Amnesty campaign continued to work for Fenian prisoners, and October 1898 saw the release 'on licence' of Thomas J Clarke, Convict No. J464, four years after his prison friend, John Daly.

Born on the Isle of Wight in 1858, son of a British soldier, Tom spent part of his childhood in South Africa. In 1865 the family returned to Dungannon, County Tyrone, where his father was appointed sergeant of the Ulster Militia. Here Tom had an opportunity to observe the poverty and emigration of a depressed area and a Catholic underclass. He grew up to embrace Irish republicanism, enrolling in the Irish Republican Brotherhood in 1878. It was John Daly, acting as the IRB Head Centre for Connacht, who enrolled him, but they were not to meet again for five years.

Clarke emigrated to the USA in 1880, and joined Clan na Gael as Daly had done. When a call was issued for single men to volunteer for the dynamite campaign in Britain, Clarke, then aged twenty-five, came forward, and was sent to Birmingham. Detectives shadowed him from his arrival, forewarned that trouble was planned, and Clarke was arrested in April, 1883, with a portmanteau containing 'an india-rubber stocking full of a liquid stated to be a dangerous explosive'. He had been observed to buy an india-rubber bag at Cow, Hill and Co., Cheapside, in London.[31]

Clarke was tried with five other IRB suspects at the Old Bailey, London, in June, under the Treason-Felony Act of

1848. He was using the alias 'Henry Hammond Wilson', and was known by this name throughout his trial and his fifteen-year imprisonment. Because of this, his family only learned in 1885 where he was, and his sister Maria could then apply for permission to visit him.[32]

Despite the punishing regime at Portland and Chatham prisons, Clarke and Daly developed a close friendship, and invented many ingenious ways of communicating with one another. Sheets of toilet paper and scraps of lead were utilised, as well as a system of Morse code, knocking against tables and cell walls. Daly managed to produce an annual newsletter every Christmas, which made its way round the jail. This friendship probably did more than anything else to keep them sane, and it was obviously very difficult for Tom when his friend was released in 1896 and he was left behind.

When Tom was released in 1898, he went first to stay with his mother Mary (née Palmer) and his sister Hanna, in Dublin. Maria Jane, his other sister, had emigrated to the USA, under the protection of Clan na Gael, where she became Mrs Teddy Fleming. His father, James, had claimed his discharge from the army in 1868, aged thirty-nine, and was given a pension of two shillings a day and admitted to the Royal Hospital, Chelsea, as a Chelsea Pensioner. He died in 1894, four years before his son's release.[33]

John Daly was most pressing in his invitations to Limerick,

and Tom duly made his way there to be presented with the Freedom of Limerick in March, 1899. He was greeted with great affection and excitement, not only by John but by all of the family. Tom, often later seen as a bitter and austere man, blossomed in the warm and lively atmosphere of the household, and displayed an unexpected aptitude for practical jokes, pinching the sisters whenever he visited the bakery shop. It must have been an extraordinary change from those endless years of grim deprivation.

One Daly girl took a particular interest in him – Kathleen, then aged twenty-one. They started writing to one another after Tom's first Limerick visit, and when he joined the family in Kilkee later that summer, they would go for romantic rambles along the cliffs in the early mornings. By the end of the summer they were engaged. Kathleen's mother was opposed to the idea – Tom was forty years old, prematurely aged by his prison experiences, and without a career or any prospects of one. But Kathleen was determined, and they were finally married in 1901 in New York, where Tom had returned to the arms of Clan na Gael.

Other family changes took place. Eileen married in 1905, and her husband, Edward (Ned) O'Toole, moved in with the Dalys until the young couple found a home of their own. Ned's grandmother, Margaret, died in 1903, aged ninety-five. A particularly sad death was that of his sister Annie, aged twenty-one, who died in Barrington's Hospital in July 1908 from typhus. John Daly himself suffered from gallstones and appendicitis in 1908, and was brought to Charlemont Street Hospital, in Dublin. He seems never to have fully recovered, and within a couple of years he was in a wheelchair.[34]

Chapter Two

• • • • • •

1906–1915

A Dream Realised

When Ned Daly left the Christian Brothers school in 1906, aged fifteen, his uncle decided that he should work in Daly's Bakery. Letters from Tom Clarke to John Daly in summer 1905 reveal that John was considering sending Ned to America for a year, to attend St Anthony's school in Greenpoint, New York.[1] Nothing came of this, however, and instead Ned spent a year at Leamy's School, doing commercial training, presumably accountancy and clerical studies. This institution, founded by a layman in 1880, later became the Crescent Clothing Factory, and is now the Frank McCourt Museum. The professor there said that Ned was 'a brilliant boy', but had no aptitude for study.[2]

John then sent him to the Royal Technical College, Glasgow, to study bakery, confectionery and breadmaking, from 1907 to 1908. The school provided 'three ovens of the most modern type, viz: − a one-sack hot-air drawplate oven, a Vienna oven, and a Scotch peel oven', and the annual fee was six guineas. Ned was awarded second-class certificates of merit in all his subjects, meaning he achieved marks of 60−80 per cent.[3] However, his health apparently came against him. He came home after a year without finishing his training, and a Glasgow doctor advised John that the heated and dusty atmosphere of a bakery would be unsuitable for Ned's constitution. It was all for nothing anyway; the Limerick Bakers' Society informed John that they would not accept Ned into the shop, probably because he was not the son of a baker. The vote, taken on 4 August 1909, went 21 for, 27 against.[4]

Ned started as a clerk in Spaight's Timber Yard, where his father Edward had once worked.[5] After two years there, he entered his uncle's bakery as a clerk, but this only lasted for a year. Relations between himself and John were poor; the old axiom about Daly males seemed to manifest itself again as Ned reached manhood, and they had many rows. This caused dissension in the rest of the family; Madge Daly was John's champion, and Laura was Ned's. John's health meanwhile continued to deteriorate. Tom Clarke, writing to John Devoy in February 1911, describes John as being in Dublin 'in Dr Sigerson's hands for treatment of his legs, which have "gone back" on him badly. He is stopping with me and excepting for his legs he is in splendid shape.'[6]

A correspondent from Butte, Montana, recalled meeting

John Daly around 1910–11, and quoted him as follows:

> 'The girls are everything that their father could have wished, and inherit his spirit. But the boy, he's a "mollycoddle". He does not seem to be made of the real stuff. His mother, I think, spoiled him and made a sissy of him.' I remember the words well now. Edward Daly was only eighteen years of age then and was what we would call a very gentlemanly or rather ladylike kind of young fellow.[7]

Ned Daly was suspected of spending time with 'low company', and is described as 'swapping pigeons in Schoolhouse Lane'.[8]

One of Ned's main interests was music; he had an excellent baritone, and would later consider being trained by Vincent O'Brien, notable for having trained John McCormack. Ned would join his pals in Limerick's only music shop in O'Connell Street (in the Coliseum Building, now a theatre) every Saturday. Here they could listen on the most up-to-date gramophone to recordings from McCormack and Caruso. At parties, he had a fine repertoire of Irish folksongs and the light opera of Gilbert and Sullivan, great favourites of all the family. But Ned's professed ambition was to be a soldier, and he would buy and study manuals on warcraft and strategy. In the absence of any army he could join (the British army was of course unthinkable), this ambition looked unlikely to be achieved.

In 1913, following a final row with his uncle, Ned Daly left Limerick and came to Dublin, where he lodged with his sister Kathleen and her husband, Tom Clarke. Here he procured another job, began to make new friends, and found himself part of a circle of revolutionary activity. This culminated in the foundation of the Irish Volunteers, and the fulfilment of his ambition to become a soldier.

Tom and Kathleen had lived in the USA until 1907, first in Brooklyn and later on a farm in Long Island, which John Daly had financed. Tom was very active in New York's Clan na Gael movement, but he was restless. He knew republicanism was gaining ground in Ireland, and wanted to play a part in any movement there. He eventually persuaded Kathleen, with difficulty, to return to Ireland with their five-year-old son John Daly Clarke. They opened a tobacconist shop in 55 Amiens Street, Dublin, and later another at 75a Parnell Street. Kathleen helped to manage both shops, and they had two more children, Tom junior in 1908 and Emmet in 1910. By 1910 they had moved from 55 Amiens Street to number 77, a shop with a house overhead.

The young Ned Daly, escaping from his uncle's disapproval and the limited opportunities for employment in Limerick, had by now come of age, and must have wanted to start making his own way. There had been some final row, and Ned may have been essentially thrown out. It was probably far more personal than political, though we have little idea of Ned's politics at this time. Tom was fond of Ned, though inclined to agree with John's opinion of this unsatisfactory nephew.

Kathleen loved her young brother, of course, but occasionally found him exasperating. He was inclined to criticise the way she let her sons play in the streets with the local children, becoming dirty and untidy and picking up a Dublin accent. A busy woman, trying to look after two shops and three sons without the domestic help the family in Limerick would have taken for granted, she had little patience with this kind of comment. It is true that her sisters, on their visits to Dublin, considered that Kathleen had let her standards slip rather too far, and they reported that she used to smack her children often. She had a lot of responsibilities, a low income, and a husband who spent much of his time plotting revolution, so a certain shortness of temper would be understandable.

Ned spent three months working as a clerk at Brooks Thomas Building Contractors, then moved to May Roberts Wholesale Chemists, Westmoreland Street.[9] Clerking and accounts were dull work for someone who longed to be a soldier, and Ned must have been quite frustrated. He was often observed at the old bookshops and stalls along the Dublin quays, examining army maps, and manuals on military strategy.[10] Letters between Tom and John Daly never mention him at all – the final row must have been devastating, and Tom obviously felt that John did not want his nephew mentioned.

43

Among all the tender back-and-forth enquiries as to the girls in Limerick and Tom's sons in Dublin, and chat about mutual friends and politics, Ned's name does not appear.[11]

As Tom had hoped, matters were indeed moving on the republican front, along with a growing emphasis on Irish cultural nationalism. The earliest and most influential of the new nationalist organisations was the Gaelic Athletic Association (GAA), founded in 1884 to preserve and develop Irish sports such as hurling and Gaelic football. The Gaelic League, which aimed to preserve Irish language and culture, had been founded in 1893, and between 1905 and 1908 the journalist Arthur Griffith developed an organisation called Sinn Féin ('We ourselves'), which had the political aim of re-establishing an independent parliament for Ireland, and a protectionist economic policy.

Maud Gonne, the glamorous young firebrand who had lectured in the USA with John Daly, marked the year 1900 by starting a women's group called Inghinidhe na hÉireann, Daughters of Ireland. This group opposed Home Rule, which John Redmond and the Irish Parliamentary Party were working towards in the British parliament. On a more militant note, Bulmer Hobson, a northern republican, established Na Fianna Éireann, a republican youth movement, with Countess Constance Markievicz, in 1909. The boys were given military training, and had to promise never to join the British army.

As a noted Fenian who had suffered for his country, Tom Clarke quickly became a focus of republican activity on his return to Dublin. He had many contacts in the north of Ireland such as Bulmer Hobson, Ernest Blythe, Denis McCullough and Seán MacDiarmada, all republican activists. Bulmer and Seán became Tom's two closest friends and allies, and joined him in developing the IRB in Dublin. He started a newspaper, *Irish Freedom*, in 1910, with financial help from John Daly and Pat McCartan, another Northern republican, and the gradual movement towards a rising can be dated from about this time.

Living with the Clarkes, Ned made friends with Seán MacDiarmada, who was a great favourite of the whole Daly family. Seán regarded their place in Limerick as his second home; in 1911, after he was struck down with the polio which permanently damaged his right leg, he spent some time recuperating there. He also stayed with the Dalys (now in 15 Barrington Street) after his release from prison in 1915, where he had served four months with hard labour under the Defence of the Realm Act for making a seditious speech in County Galway. He and John Daly became the best of friends, despite their age difference. From prison, he wrote to John:

> Many a time during the few months I have had here have I thought how I would enjoy a game of bridge with you when I got out, while I smoked one of your good cigars

and maybe sampled a little drop out of that big bottle of the wine of the country.[12]

Young Ned Daly was still not earning enough to live independently. He was stuck in an unexciting job, with few prospects of advancement, and denied the one ambition he ever took seriously. Family sources confirm that he was considering emigration to the United States, with the intention of joining the US army. If he could not serve his own country, he might be of use elsewhere. However, all this changed dramatically in November 1913, when the Irish Volunteers were founded at a meeting held in the Rotunda Rink, Dublin.

The growing nationalist mood of the country had been enraged by the foundation in the north of the Ulster Volunteers, who were vowed to oppose Home Rule. The British authorities seemed to be allowing this force to carry arms and to parade openly. It was obviously necessary to counter this with a nationalist army, to defend the Home Rule Bill which was coming forward, and to prevent Ulster from detaching itself from the rest of the country.

The IRB had been infiltrating all of the nationalist movements, manoeuvring their members into positions of influence. Men such as Clarke and MacDiarmada did not want to be openly involved with this new organisation; they were known revolutionaries, and would have made the British authorities suspicious. The IRB definitely had plans for the

Volunteers, but first large numbers of men had to be encouraged to join; it did not matter yet whether these volunteers were merely interested in defending Home Rule, or were really hoping for violent revolution. IRB men were fitted into key positions in the Volunteers all over the country.

The northern IRB member Bulmer Hobson put himself forward as secretary of the Provisional Committee of the Volunteers. Eoin MacNeill, professor of Early and Medieval Irish History at University College Dublin, and a founder member of the Gaelic League, became chief-of-staff; he was not an IRB member.

Kathleen Clarke writes:

> The [first] meeting, held on November 25th, 1913, was a huge success. The Rotunda was packed and there was a big overflow meeting ... I never saw a happier young man than he [Ned] was the night he joined. He told me it was what he had always been wishing for.[13]

The rink held about 7,000, and up to 5,000 more thronged the Concert Hall and the gardens outside. Ned joined B Company, First Battalion, as a private, but when elections were held for officers, he was appointed captain. He was very young for this promotion, and it may have had something to do with his relationship with IRB leaders such as Clarke and MacDiarmada, as well as his own qualities.

The night the Volunteers were founded, Ned was introduced

to James O'Sullivan (usually Jim, or Séamus), aged twenty-two, who was to become his closest friend, although a more extrovert character. A rare photograph of Ned out of uniform shows the two friends relaxed and laughing together, in civilian clothes, possibly out 'on the town'. Jim worked in a grocer's shop, but strove to improve his education; he would read second-hand books from the city bookstalls during his spare time, often in the peaceful surroundings of Glasnevin Cemetery.[14] He had been a member of the Boys' Brigade, a Protestant organisation established to 'drill and discipline' wayward boys, and this quasi-military training meant that he was elected 1st lieutenant of B Company.

Both young men were now in charge of men mostly older and more experienced than they, and they grew moustaches to make themselves look older, without much success.[15] Ned seems to have dealt with the situation by adopting an aloof and reserved manner on parade; he may have feared that the men would not accept his authority otherwise. Yet, the men he commanded all seem to have respected him greatly, and admired him as the consummate soldier. He was not tall, and had a spare, slight figure, but nonetheless he commanded respect.

Speaking of Ned Daly years later, one of his men, Johnny O'Connor, called him:

> ... a quiet unassuming man, who was a real stickler for form.
> He always believed that everything should be done properly,

Right: Ned Daly as a young man.

Below: Daly sisters and Ned, in 1901. Standing: Nora, Annie, Agnes, Carrie, Laura. Seated: Eileen (O'Toole), Kathleen, Madge, Edward.

Above: Daly family, 1894, l-r, standing: Catharine Daly, James, Lollie, Jim Jones, Eileen, Madge; l-r, seated: Nora, Edward ('Ned'), Agnes, Mrs Margaret Daly, Kathleen, Laura; on floor, seated: Carrie, Annie.

Left: Members of the Daly family outside Clonlong.

Above: Daly family at Kilkee *c*1901. Ned as a boy can be seen just off centre, wearing a cap.

Below: John Daly rowing *Lua-Tagna*, presented to him by Limerick's workingmen, 1897; l-r: Eileen, Madge, Agnes, John, Kathleen, Ned.

Left: Daly family at Clonlong, l-r Kathleen, Ned, Mrs Daly, Agnes, Nora and Annie.

Left: Jim O'Sullivan.

Above right: Daly's bakery and bill head.

Below right: Ned Daly and Jim O'Sullivan.

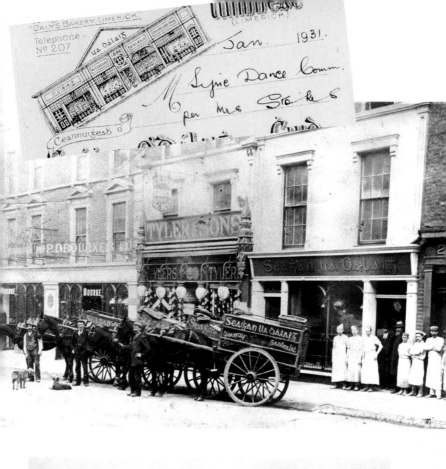

Left: Ned Daly in formal evening wear.

Below: Ned Daly (seated, right) and friend.

Above: Edward Daly senior.

Left: John Daly, Fenian, before his imprisonment.

Above: O'Donovan Rossa funeral passing St Stephen's Green, 1 August 1915. Ned Daly can be seen as lone uniformed figure directly behind the hearse.

Left: Tom Clarke.

but I don't think, in giving an instruction, he ever raised his voice. He wasn't the bullying type, but a whisper from him was as good as a bark from anybody else. There was never a more perfect gentleman that I have met than Ned Daly.[16]

As captain of B Company, he brought it to a high pitch of discipline and efficiency in a remarkably short time, according to a later assessment of his command. On route marches he would help to keep up the spirits of his men by singing 'Eileen Og', which became the regimental song of the First Battalion.

Ned took full part in the fun and social life of the Volunteer fundraising dances, but impressed on his men that 'B' Company meant 'Business'[17]. A letter from an old friend to Jim O'Sullivan, some years later, reminisced fondly of 'the glorious days when "B of the 1st was it".'[18]

A women's auxiliary, Cumann na mBan, was established in April 1914, and all the Daly sisters (apart from Eileen, now a young mother) became involved. Kathleen Clarke and Áine Ceannt, wife of Éamonn, started the Central Branch in Dublin. The members were trained in drilling, signalling, home nursing and first aid; training also included the care and use of arms. Branches were founded in every county, growing and spreading in tandem with the development of the Volunteers.

Madge Daly became President of the Limerick City branch, a position she held until 1924. This branch started first-aid classes, with a grant from the Department of Education; the money from this grant was, of course, passed directly to the Arms' Fund of the Irish Volunteers. In that way, Madge gloated, the British government was unwittingly subscribing to the funds of its enemies.[19]

By March 1914, the Irish Volunteers numbered 20,000. This rose to 50,000 after the first reading of the Home Rule Bill, in May, and had doubled to 100,000 by June. At this stage John Redmond, leader of the Irish Parliamentary Party, who had been viewing the development of this military force with some anxiety, insisted that the Volunteers should be brought under the control of the IPP. He was suspicious that the IRB was influencing it, and was worried that the Volunteers could be used to oppose the Home Rule Bill. The IRB had expected such a development, but Redmond won out for the time being; the IPP took control of half of the seats on the Executive Committee.

Bulmer Hobson had helped Redmond in this take-over bid, against IRB interests. He was court-martialled by the Supreme Council of the IRB, and resigned his seat on that council. Tom Clarke never spoke to him again, thus losing one of his few close friends. IRB member Seán McGarry later said:

> I never saw him so moved ... During his life he had had many, very many grievous disappointments but this was the worst and the bitterness of it was increased by the fact that

it was brought about by a trusted friend.[20]

Writing to John Devoy on 7 July, Tom admitted:

He [Hobson] and I had been more intimate than any other
two men in this town ... It has been a terrible stab to me.

Roger Casement was another IRB member who supported allowing Redmond's nominees on the committee,
much to the annoyance of John Daly. Daly was by now
spending part of each summer in Dalkey, County Dublin,
under medical treatment, and Fionán Lynch (a captain in
F Company of the Volunteers), Seán MacDiarmada and
Gearóid O'Sullivan would join him to play bridge.

Fionán Lynch recalled:

One evening when we arrived at the house, Casement was
there before us, and he left shortly after we arrived. John
Daly turned to Seán McDermott ... and, in his great boom-
ing voice, said, 'Damn you, McDermott, you came at the
wrong time. I was just going to pitch into him'... Daly was,
however, a great realist, and he wasted no time on regrets,
but told Seán that he and his crowd should try to keep as
much control as possible through the companies.[21]

Clarke, despite the IPP setback, was jubilant at the success of
the Volunteers, and at the spirit he observed among the young
members. On its foundation, he wrote to Joe McGarrity of
Clan na Gael:

Then the drills – every drill hall packed since – too much packed to allow of satisfactory drilling – then the class of fellows who are there – and the enthusiasm and the National note in the atmosphere! 'Tis good to be in Ireland these times.[22]

Later in 1914, he wrote to John Devoy in great excitement:

Never in my recollection have I known in any former movement anything to compare with the spontaneous rush that is being made all over to get into the movement and start drill and get hold of a rifle ... And the change that has come over the young men of the country who are volunteering! Erect, heads up in the air, the glint in the eye, and then the talent and ability that had been latent and is now being discovered! Young fellows who had been regarded as something like wastrels now changed to energetic soldiers and absorbed in the work, and taking pride that at last they feel they can do something for their country that will count.[23]

He must have been picturing his nephew-in-law as he wrote this romantic passage.

Meanwhile, Ned was progressing in his new career, which seemed to fit him like a glove. According to Éamonn Dore (who later married Ned's sister Nora):

... he developed a taste for study foreign to his earlier life. Everything of a military nature he, as it were, devoured voraciously, and his retentive memory for such was the wonder of his fellow Brigadier officers.

Meeting his mother, who was on a holiday in Kingstown [Dún Laoghaire, Dublin], he asked her to pray for his success in his exam. She had not heard previously of this exam, was overjoyed at, as she thought, his ambition to get on materially in the world: a trait which she knew up to this to be foreign to his character. On asking what exam she got as a reply: 'Captain of my company in the Irish Volunteers'.[24]

There are several descriptions of Ned in his new incarnation. PJ Stephenson, a member of D Company of the First Battalion, wrote:

Daly was a fine figure of a man with a rather serious looking face and sad dark eyes. In his well-tailored green uniform he looked every inch a soldier. The combination of the soldierly figure with the pale complexion and the dark moustache created havoc among the ladies, while his smart military bearing inspired great respect in the minds of the rank and file of the Battalion.[25]

Republican and Volunteer Liam Ó Briain described the two comrades:

[He and Jim] would walk the streets of the city ... both proudly wearing the uniforms of Óglaigh na h-Éireann [Irish Volunteers], swords held smartly by their sides, and

English soldiers would salute them thinking they were officers of their own.[26]

The officers of the Volunteers would attend Cumann na mBan meetings, coming from Foresters' Hall in Parnell Square, the Volunteer HQ. Dr Brigid Lyons Thornton of Cumann na mBan remembered him well:

> [W]e had Commandant Daly ... He was very austere, very withdrawn, I thought, but a man you would never forget. He would come in and sit around and talk to some people who knew him and with [Captain] O'Sullivan.[27]

She was thrilled with him and felt that although he was quiet he was very forceful.

> What I felt about him ... and also about Séamus Sullivan – they probably would not care to be told this – was that they were the nearest approach to British officers in appearance and inspired us girls with feelings of enthusiasm and caused us many heart throbs.[28]

From Jim O'Sullivan's later reminiscences to his sons, it is clear that the two lads were well aware of the effects they were having, and had a good eye for the girls themselves.

Ned also joined the Keating Branch of the Gaelic League, and probably attended some of their weekly history lectures. That particular city-centre branch seems to have been used mostly as a meeting place for the Volunteers, whose most prominent leaders were members of it.

In April 1914, the Ulster Volunteers acquired arms through an illegal gun-running at Larne, County Antrim. The Irish Volunteer leaders vowed to organise a similar mission, and on 26 July 1914 a shipload of arms arrived in Howth, County Dublin on the yacht *Asgard*. About a week later a similar landing in Kilcoole, County Wicklow, delivered the rest. The total amounted to about 1,600 Mauser rifles and 46,000 rounds of ammunition.

Edward Daly headed his company as the Volunteers made a route march to Howth on 26 July. Arriving there, they unloaded the rifles with the help of senior members of the Fianna, and the account of Captain Seán Prendergast of C Company gives an excellent idea of the excitement as rifle after rifle was unpacked from its straw and handed out: 'We were frantic, hysterical ... Some men cheered, some wept with joy; some others too overcome by emotion went pale with excitement.'

Word then reached them that the authorities had been informed, and the returning Volunteers found themselves blocked by the police and some troops of the King's Own Scottish Borderers at the Howth Road junction. Ned Daly and other officers went forward to parley. Ned had told his men to pass the word along to the others to 'disappear', and gradually the Volunteers began to melt away, many hiding rifles in ditches and hedges as they went. The event immediately became legend in republican circles, says Prendergast, with tales of 'how the British warship engaged in patrolling Dublin Bay was by a clever ruse diverted to Wicklow, and that the Volunteers had cut telephonic communications with Howth'.[29]

Few Volunteers were arrested, and most of the rifles got safely away. One of the first rifles unpacked was put aside for John Daly, and Tom Clarke carried it down to Limerick for him, along with a revolver which would be easier for the old man to use. Seán MacDiarmada, describing the events to John, wrote, 'I am glad to say that Ned acted all the part of a man all day.'[30] The following week saw Ned at Kilcoole, where, in the landing of arms at this seaside village, he again distinguished himself, according to Éamonn Dore.[31]

The British troops were frustrated, and on their way back to Dublin on Bachelor's Walk, on the quays, they fired at a group of people who had jeered at them and thrown stones. Three people were killed and thirty-eight injured; the funerals turned into huge nationalist demonstrations. Rather coldbloodedly, MacDiarmada wrote to John Daly, 'The crowds in the streets have been charged several times by the military. It will do good and all is well. That ought to open the eyes of the fools as to what Liberal Government is.'[32]

The Dublin Castle administration tried to pin the blame for this debacle on the assistant commissioner of the Dublin Metropolitan Police, as his chief had been away.

However, the chief himself, Commissioner Sir John Ross, was not a man to let this happen:

> I remember seeing him [Ross], in an explosive state of pent-up rage, outside the Under Secretary's Office waiting to be admitted. At the meeting that ensued he consigned Sir James Dougherty, the Chief Secretary [Birrell] and the Government to the waste-paper basket for ineptitude and handed in his own resignation.[33]

In August 1914, England declared war on Germany. The Home Rule Act was signed into law in September, but immediately suspended until the end of the war. This caused great frustration in Ireland, even among constitutional nationalists. However, Redmond held to his path, and in a speech at Woodenbridge, County Wicklow on 20 September he urged the Irish Volunteers (now numbering about 180,000) to join the British in fighting German expansionism. The movement split; those who followed Redmond's lead, the vast majority, became known as the National Volunteers. A rump of 11,000 or so remained under the control of the IRB, which was considering how best to use this turn of events.

The republican element kept their heads down for a while, drilling the Volunteers and publishing a series of short-lived newsletters; as each was banned, another was begun, and much of this was funded by John Daly. Officers' courses were held, and lectures given on house-to-house fighting, guerrilla warfare and signalling (a speciality of the Fianna).

Arms were being purchased where possible, often from British soldiers, and special belts and bandoliers were designed. Volunteer Patrick Ramsbottom was able to buy a Martini-Henry rifle from Tom Clarke.[34] Provision of equipment was uneven; according to Liam O'Carroll of A Company, his captain, McCormack, was more interested in caps and uniforms than in arms. 'That was the one thing outstanding against him, even by Ned Daly. Every penny we had, he was always purchasing caps and badges.'

O'Carroll's father had a shop in Manor Street, and bought many Lee Enfield rifles from British army soldiers from the nearby barracks.

> These fellows, when they wanted a few drinks, would take anything out of the barracks. The usual thing was that they would bring a parcel around; and he would give them five shillings in any case; it might be a pair of old boots; it might be two .45s. On one occasion, there was delivered to him a lorry load of petrol in two-gallon tins.[35]

When Jerry Golden of B Company heard through a friendly milkman of a hoard of rifles found under the floor of a house, after the owner had died, he was able to get £10 from Ned Daly to buy them, and smuggled them away on the milkman's cart, concealed in a roll of lino. The dead man had been buying them from British soldiers, as Mr O'Carroll had done.[36]

The First Battalion carried out field work in the Dublin Mountains:'[A]t 6 am on a Sunday morning when the snow was thick on the ground ... we took part in field exercises with the Fingal Brigade,' remembered Seán Cody of C Company.[37] Test mobilisations and marches took place frequently, and the police shadowing them, mostly older men, were forced to march on the double to keep up.

One day they went for a route march, and returning after a busy day, tired but happy, the battalion began to sing 'The Watch on the Rhine'. Ned stopped them, and said that while he was appreciative of their work, and glad to hear them in good voice, he would prefer to hear them sing 'The Watch on the Liffey'. The Liffey would be their battleground before another twelve months, and he hoped every man would still be as much in earnest.[38]

Ned was still living with the Clarkes, and his social life had expanded through joining the Volunteers. Volunteer summer camps were run in 1914 and 1915, which he apparently enjoyed to the full:

When the work in drill halls was done, Ned was a happy, joyous boy, always ready for a dance or any bit of fun. He was passionately fond of music, had a fine baritone voice and a big collection of Irish songs. The evenings almost always ended in a concert. At the time he worked for a

wholesale chemist [May Roberts] who had large army con-
tracts. All the employees were expected to work overtime.
Ned absolutely refused. He wanted all his spare time for his
Volunteer work.[39]

Margaret Browne of Cumann na mBan remembers meeting him often at Ceilis (Irish dancing nights):

He used to walk home with us, also Jim Ryan who was in
his battalion. Daly gave me the impression that he was in
the Volunteers for the excitement. He seemed to keep great
discipline because one night in our digs, when it came to
the time for some Volunteer meeting, he ordered Jim Ryan
to go to it and remained on himself with us. I remember
we had only three eggs left for tea and Jim Ryan had to do
without one.[40]

It would seem that Ned was still rather a spoiled young
man!

Annie, wife of Frank Fahy, a captain in C Company, also
remembered him fondly:

We lived at Park Place, Islandbridge … Almost every Sunday
night some of the boys visited us. Seán McDermott, Ned Daly,
Séamus O'Sullivan, Con Colbert, Finn Lynch … They often
brought their friends along; we were like one happy family.[41]

Serious matters went on in the background, of course.
In November 1914 Robert Monteith, a Volunteer organiser

who worked with Roger Casement, was sacked from his job in the Ordnance Department, and served with an order to leave Dublin at once because of his republican activities. 'While the police officer was serving this order on Monteith, he was covered with a pistol by Captain Ned Daly, who lurked in the background "in case of any crooked work".'[42]

In Limerick, the Daly family was in the thick of the republican movement. John Daly donated land for a Fianna hall at the back of his home, 15 Barrington Street, and helped to pay for its erection. It was opened in 1912, complete with stage and seating accommodation. Lectures and concerts were held there, to raise funds for the national movement, and drilling was carried on; Laura, one of the Daly sisters, was in charge. It was also used by Cumann na mBan.

The British army was commandeering horses for army service overseas. Madge Daly is said to have provided revolvers to the Daly's Bakery van drivers, so they could shoot the horses rather than hand them over. Fortunately the situation did not arise.

The Daly home became a centre of republican communications. Ernest Blythe, an active Volunteer organiser, wrote:

> Old John Daly was failing very much at the time; he was not able to talk with real ease, but his prestige was enormous. His nieces were very active and the hospitality of the family was without stint. Every stranger connected with the Volunteers was invited to stay with them.[43]

Of course such a hotbed of revolution was a focus of police attention, and some unnamed friend of the family supplied information to the DMP, giving them the names of American correspondents as well as those of John Daly's visitors. None of it seems to have been of much importance; the informant was afraid to ask too many questions in case the family became suspicious.[44] The Dalys were also drawing closer to Patrick Pearse; Tom and Kathleen's eldest son, Daly, was sent to Pearse's school, St Enda's, with the approval of John and Madge (who probably paid the fees). A letter from Pearse to Madge, dated 7 March 1915, thanks her for this, and adds, 'I am glad your Uncle keeps fairly well. Won't you remember me to him? I think of him in his room waiting and watching. The two noblest memories of my life are of him and of John Devoy.'[45]

Among the items Ned Daly handed to his sisters before his execution was a wallet, empty but for a railway ticket to Limerick, dated Christmas Eve 1914. Who knows why he kept this particular ticket, but perhaps it was a souvenir of the first time he was able to return to Limerick since leaving it in anger. As a Volunteer captain, and showing great promise as a soldier, he was probably welcomed back at last by his formidable uncle John.

Around this time we find the first hint of a change in Ned Daly's personal life. Although he could be the life and soul of the party, few people ever seemed to come close to him, and the lack of any written material apart from a handful of letters maintains that deep privacy. He has been described as 'shy and sensitive [as a lad] and strangely silent in a home full of children, in a way self-sufficient and uncommunicative except with his mother'.[46]

However, in a letter to his sister Laura (undated, but internal evidence indicates that it was written in early 1915), he thanks her for agreeing to act as a confidante to him, and proceeds to explain his secret further:

> We are going to be formally engaged at end of March, when this term ends ... She has been offered a two-year extension and has refused it as it means italian opera at Convent Garden [sic], instead of that, if we can't get married soon after July, she has a notion of taking a part in some musical comedy, which would be easy enough to get ...
>
> She asked me if you would write her, she says she wants to tell you things. Well if you will, the address is Miss Molly Keegan, 52 Holland Rd, Kensington, London West. Do write, won't you. You know she saw your photo and likes you a lot and I'm sure you will like her ... I would like to bring Molly down at Easter for the few days. Do you think it might be done. There's another thing, too I must tell you, she's thoroughly Irish and if the necessity was there and I didn't go it would finish me with her ...
>
> PS. Do you think I'd better tell Mamma. I think I ought to you know.

To the researcher, this comes out of the blue. All the descriptions of Ned Daly in a social context put him with groups, or with Jim O'Sullivan, but no one ever links him with any particular girl. So who was Molly Keegan?

Maryanne Margaret Keegan, known as Molly, was a gifted mezzo-soprano singer who in 1912, aged nineteen, won a Gold Medal at the Feis Ceoil, a music festival held annually in Dublin. She also won the Ladies' Committee Prize of a year's tuition in the Royal College of Music, London.[47] She remained there for three years, having won a further open scholarship for two years.[48]

She was clearly a very talented singer, as the glowing reviews of her performances attest. In the reviews of the Prizewinners' concert, published on 13 May 1912, the critic of the *Freeman's Journal* said: 'In "The Deserted Maiden" (Macalister) she showed to advantage real dramatic power besides the great range and magnificent tone she possesses', and the *Daily Express* speaks of her fine dramatic soprano voice, which 'gives promise of a brilliant future'. There was a moment of controversy when JC Doyle, a music teacher, wrote to the newspapers complaining that her training had been credited to a well-known Dublin music professor, Randal Woodhouse. Instead, Mr Doyle protested, *he* had been Molly Keegan's only tutor for the previous two years, and was responsible for her many prizes at the Sligo Feis and the Father Mathew Feis. Mr Woodhouse retorted instantly that he had taught her the song she sang best ('The Deserted Maiden'), and had been responsible for her earliest musical development, on which Mr Doyle had 'put a dash of whitewash'.[49]

The Keegan family is listed in the 1911 Census, at 33 St Peter's Road, West Side, Phibsboro (Glasnevin District). Molly lived there with her widowed mother and her brother William, then aged sixteen. The head of the household was her mother's brother, John Patrick Sweeney, a widower with two children, and the other family member was John's brother William, a bachelor. The Sweeney siblings had all been born in County Waterford. John was an overseer in the Telegraph Dept (GPO), and William was a clerk in the Dublin United Tramway Company.

Unfortunately, no more can be said of Molly Keegan in relation to Ned Daly. His closest friend James O'Sullivan never spoke of her, or seemed to have met her, and his sister Laura knew little apart from the mention in the letter. It is not known where or how the couple met; if Molly had attended the Gaelic League, other friends of Ned's would have been aware of the romance, so the link between them was probably musical. Most likely it was the Feis Ceoil, because Ned, with an interest in singing, may have attended the competitions and the prizewinning concerts, although he is not known to have been a competitor himself.

Since Molly went to London in late 1912, some months

before Ned moved to Dublin, and stayed there for three years, only coming home during term breaks, opportunities to meet were surely very limited. Ned never travelled out of Ireland, as far as is known. If the letter mentioning her had not been preserved, no one would ever have known of this connection. It is possible that he was reading more into the relationship than actually existed, but there is something very definite about that reference to a formal engagement. Although Ned was about to become a commandant, in charge of up to four hundred men, the letter is that of a young and uncertain boy, seeking his sister's approval and nervous about telling his mamma.

When asked about Molly Keegan years later, Laura told her children that Molly's family had not approved of the Volunteer connection, and had somehow separated the pair. However, Molly certainly went to London to follow her musical career, rather than being 'packed off', as Laura implied. The relationship probably foundered on political differences. Molly's father and grandfather had been members of the Royal Irish Constabulary (RIC), which her brother also joined when he grew up, so she had a constitutional nationalist background. She may have suddenly realised that Ned was not just dressing up as a soldier for fun, but was seriously planning armed revolution. Since she married a Welsh businessman, Frederick G Harries, in London in February 1916, her relationship with Ned must have come to an end during 1915. Widowed in 1936, she remarried in 1937; she had no children from either marriage.[50]

In early 1915, Ned Daly looked for someone who knew the counties around Dublin – Meath, Kildare, Wicklow – and Jerry Golden volunteered. He was able to assure Ned that he could find his way anywhere in these counties by the shortest route. Ned told him that he himself was about to be appointed commandant, and would be forwarding despatches to other parts of the country, so he needed someone reliable. Golden was also useful because he held a gun licence, and could get hold of sporting cartridges, for which Daly gave him money from time to time. Golden worried that all his courier work was causing him to miss drill and training, but his commandant assured him that the work he was doing was just as valuable.

At Whitsun, May 1915, Ned Daly found himself back in Limerick again. As a commandant, having been appointed on 30 January 1915, he was now in charge of about 400 men. This further promotion was probably completely on his own merits. He was immediately sworn into the IRB, and co-opted onto a sub-committee of the Military Council. It would have been considered dangerous to have him living in the same house as Clarke, when rebellion was being planned, if he had not taken the IRB oath. Piaras Béaslaí, Daly's second-in-command, remembered:

> My diary shows that on Feb. 13th, 1915 … [Daly] called me
> out to 'propound a certain plan'. This must be the plan for
> the First Battalion. I remember he first told me of it out-
> side Tom Clarke's shop. On a later date he again spoke of
> the subject and gave me maps of the Broadstone and Four
> Courts area which, I understood, he had received from his
> committee – or, in other words, the Military Council.[51]

The visit to Limerick was a fund-raising and recruiting exercise for the Limerick Battalion, and Volunteers from Dublin,
Cork and Tipperary were to parade in full equipment. Patrick
Pearse, Seán MacDiarmada, Terence MacSwiney and Tomás
MacCurtain were among those who marched, about 1,200 in
all. Information reached the Limerick Battalion that a hostile
reception was being arranged, but it was not expected to
amount to much.

The Volunteers were not popular in Limerick, which was
a 'garrison town', containing numerous British troops with
their families. These saw the Volunteers as traitors to Britain,
with their pockets full of German gold. At Wolfe Tone Street,
the soldiers in New Barracks were vocal in their contempt,
but the loudest verbal barrage came from the 'separation
women', the wives of soldiers fighting in the trenches. At
Mungret Street, attacks escalated from words to deeds, with
bricks, stones, bottles and cabbage-stumps being flung at
the marching Volunteers. Later, it was learned that mysteri-
ous sums of money had provided certain sections of the

population with alcohol. The intent may have been to provoke the Volunteers to fire on civilians, which would lead to the organisation being banned.

Military discipline and training prevailed, and the battered Volunteers reached the Fianna Hall for refreshments in good order, presuming the worst was over. However, 'bands of intoxicated rowdies' roamed the streets, attacking Volunteers while the RIC stood by.[52] A young boy was hit on the head by a bottle thrown by a civilian, and rumour spread that he had been shot by the 'Sinn Féiners'. Hundreds of angry men and women headed for the railway station, to catch the Volunteers as they tried to leave the city. The Limerick Battalion, appalled at the way in which their national leaders were being treated, were about to rush on the crowd when some of the local Catholic clergy succeeded in calming the situation. A number of guns had been whipped from the hands of retreating Volunteers, but most of these were subsequently recovered.

Writing to Madge Daly from St Enda's on 28 May 1915, Patrick Pearse remarked:

I hope our visit has helped the Limerick Company. We all felt that the great bulk of the people in the city were sympathetic and that the hostile element was small though noisy. Personally, I found the whole experience useful.[53]

Michael Brennan of the Limerick Battalion remembered:

When all the visitors had got away, a number of us were having tea at Daly's. Tom Clarke came in looking ruffled and weary and sat in a corner of the room with his head resting on his hand. He declined tea and said nothing for half an hour or so. Then he straightened up and snapped, 'I've always wondered why King William couldn't take Limerick. I know now.'[54]

Ned Daly had managed his battalion competently during this riot. He was now about to step onto a larger stage, a massive IRB funeral for the Fenian hero, Jeremiah O'Donovan Rossa.

Chapter Three

• • • • • • •

1915–16

Preparations

For Fenian sympathisers, Jeremiah O'Donovan Rossa was a legend. Sentenced to penal servitude in 1865, he smuggled a letter from prison which described the treatment the Fenian prisoners were receiving. The resulting controversy led to an amnesty campaign, and O'Donovan Rossa was among a number of Fenians released in January 1871, under the condition of exile from Britain.

He headed for the United States, and in September 1875 he and Patrick Ford, editor of the New York paper *Irish World*, launched a 'skirmishing fund', which was to finance a dynamiting campaign in British cities, although Clan na Gael deplored the risk of bad publicity. A series of attacks took place in Lancashire and London in 1881, and the campaign culminated in bomb explosions in Westminster and the Tower of London in 1885. It was this campaign which led to the arrests of Tom Clarke in 1883 and John Daly in 1884.

O'Donovan Rossa spent the rest of his life in America, but vowed that he would be buried in Ireland. When he died in New York on 30 June 1915, aged eighty-three, the IRB leadership in Dublin immediately saw the possibility of a set-piece nationalist event, a great opportunity for propaganda. Devoy cabled to Tom Clarke, 'Rossa dead, what shall we do?' Tom cabled back, 'Send his body home at once,' and said to his wife, 'If Rossa had planned to die at the most opportune time for serving his country, he could not have done better.'[1]

A large committee, with numerous sub-committees, planned the funeral, ostensibly under the auspices of the Wolfe Tone Memorial Association. This was an open organisation through which the IRB sometimes acted. The funeral was to consist of a massive procession, moving through Dublin city centre to Glasnevin Cemetery. Thomas MacDonagh designed the general plan, and Clarke was the prime mover:

During the few weeks preceding the funeral his energy seemed to be inexhaustible and the plans for the route and the dispositions of the various participating bodies which appeared in the papers were actually drawn by himself on the counter in his shop.[2]

Tom wrote to Madge Daly to invite her to attend:

Come up for the funeral it will be worth attending – we are getting out a souvenir of it – all our best writers engaged on the work. Oh God if Uncle John were only able to be with us in these times – Many and many a time I regret that he is knocked out – He would be worth a whole army corps of the ordinary workers.[3]

Finally, Tom granted the honour of giving the funeral oration to Patrick Pearse: 'Make it as hot as hell, throw discretion to the winds.'[4]

The funeral was planned for 1 August. Rossa's widow and daughter sailed to Liverpool on 19 July, and were escorted to Dublin by a group including Kathleen Clarke. The body of Jeremiah O'Donovan Rossa reached Dublin a couple of days later. The remains spent a night in the Pro-Cathedral, Dublin, then were brought to lie in state in City Hall. The coffin was guarded day and night by Irish Volunteers, from Ned Daly's First Battalion, and thousands of people paid their respects.

The funeral procession consisted of fully-armed detachments of Volunteers from all over the country, along with Cumann na mBan, James Connolly's Irish Citizen Army and contingents of young men from the GAA.

The whole fitted together, forming a complete and finished scheme which, on the day of the funeral, despite the tremendous magnitude of this national act of homage, worked without a hitch.[5]

Captain James O'Sullivan was in charge of the Guard of Honour.[6]

The funeral of Jeremiah O'Donovan Rossa is best remembered, of course, for the stunning and carefully crafted speech made by Patrick Pearse at the conclusion of the ceremony. The authorities could only stand by impotently, taking notes, as sheer sedition was spoken over the open grave:

> I propose to you then that, here by the grave of this unrepentant Fenian ... we ask of God, each one for himself, such unshakable purpose, such high and gallant courage, such unbreakable strength of soul as belonged to O'Donovan Rossa ...
>
> The Defenders of this Realm have worked well in secret and in the open. They think that they have purchased half of us and intimidated the other half. They think that they have foreseen everything, think that they have provided against everything; but the fools, the fools, the fools! – they have left us our Fenian dead, and while Ireland holds these graves, Ireland unfree shall never be at peace.

Pearse had certainly followed Clarke's instructions to the letter. As the Funeral Souvenir recounted, '... there was an intense, all-pervading, silence, then we gave forth round after round of cheers which surely must have gladdened the spirits of Rossa and his colleagues ... who lie so near.' The whole event was so impressive that it inspired many of the spectators to commit themselves to the republican cause. Leslie Price, later Bean de Barra, 'suddenly realised that the men I had seen ... looked as if they meant serious business ... the following Thursday night I joined the Ard Craobh of the Cumann na mBan.'[7]

This was also a big day for Edward Daly, as the First Battalion took a leading role in the procession. Photographs show him leading his battalion, with his perfect uniform and highly-polished boots, gleaming sword erect, every inch the young officer. In a photograph of the Funeral Committee, he can be seen sitting in the front row, close to Tom Clarke, and was obviously completely trusted by this time.

An anonymous account of Edward Daly published much later in the *Limerick Leader* (26 May 1934) states that around this time the British government began to press firms to encourage their young employees to enlist. A manager in May Roberts interviewed Ned Daly, offering him a commission in the British army, but Ned indignantly refused and was dismissed. The account goes on to say that his uncle agreed that he should not seek other employment but concentrate instead on his Volunteer activity. This would imply that John Daly provided an income for him instead.

However, one of the few letters extant written by Ned Daly gives a different account. In an undated letter to his favourite sister Laura, he says:

> I am leaving M.R. on Sat. I can't give you the main reason here, but it was only partly a question of screw [wages]. I'm jolly glad anyhow – I should have done it anyhow. I have one or two things in view but nothing definite yet.

In the letter to Laura of early 1915 in which he had revealed his relationship with Molly Keegan, he had also described an argument with his boss about the level of his wages and the amount of work he was expected to do, so relations had obviously not been good.

As the IRB plans for the Rising advanced, all the commandants were advised to leave their places of work in order to concentrate on arrangements, and this could be the real reason Ned abandoned May Roberts and Company. This appears to have happened early in 1916, but the whole issue is unclear. Éamonn Dore says that Ned had left his job by mid-January 1916.[8]

Ned might have also been considering a singing career. In a letter to Laura dated 12 October 1915, he says:

> By the bye, tell Mamma to hang on to that cash for the present, you see some people that I know have told me recently that I am a big fool not to get my voice trained and have advised me to get expert opinion from Vincent O'Brien. I am going to see him some day this week. He is the man that trained McCormack and would not touch a voice unless 'twas good. So I will see what he says. He's pretty stiff in his prices though.

We don't know if this approach was ever made.

Ned spent Christmas 1915 in Limerick with the family. There

were twenty-two people in the Daly home that Christmas, including the Clarkes, James O'Sullivan, Con Colbert and Seán MacDiarmada. The two maids vanished on Christmas morning, leaving a note on the table, so everyone had to turn to. Madge left the cutlery on the table, and came back to find Tom trying to lay it out properly, muttering, 'Well, I know they go in a straight line anyway ...' James and Con insisted on doing the washing–up, boasting about their army–camp experience, but the crashing sounds from the kitchen were not reassuring.

Censorship of the mail of John Daly and the Clarkes had been rescinded early in 1915, since it was obvious that any important correspondence was not going through the regular post.[9] However, they were still persons of interest, and were followed around Limerick by the RIC. In the reports, Clarke is described as 'sallow, dark eyes, thin visage, thin nose, slight make, abscess mark on right jaw, hair and moustache dark, turning grey', and James O'Sullivan as 'medium active make, fresh complexion, long features, long nose, dark hair, small brown moustache'.[10] None of the RIC lists of people being followed include Ned Daly, but many important RIC records of that period are missing.

Back in Dublin in early 1916, the Supreme Council of the IRB 'definitely voted that we would fight at the earliest date possible'. Clarke confirmed this to Madge Daly, who was in Dublin, and gave her details of the plans to take back to

Uncle John.[11] He also gave her money for the commandant of the Limerick Volunteers, Michael Colivet.

The historian Joe Lee, discussing the date of the Rising, dismisses the notion that a 'blood sacrifice' was planned. If that is all you want, there is no need to plan it meticulously, over twenty months, and maintain the utmost secrecy while doing so. The IRB leaders cannot have known how long the Great War would last, but must have concluded that it would be at least long enough to allow them to lay careful plans. This was no mad headlong rush into the cannon's mouth, or at least it was not intended to be so.[12]

From early 1916, preparations for the Rising continued apace. Ned Daly and Jim O'Sullivan walked the area around the Four Courts, planning their defences. Eoin MacNeill, chief-of-staff of the Irish Volunteers, still unaware of the IRB plans for an armed rebellion, maintained to the Volunteer executive that such a rebellion would only be justified if there were any chance of ultimate success, and that Britain's military dominance made this utterly unlikely. However, he added, 'I have not the slightest doubt on the point that we are morally and in every way justified in keeping by all necessary force all arms as we have got or can get.'

On 19 January 1916, James Connolly disappeared for four days. The full details of this episode have never been clear, but it would appear that the IRB Military Council had decided to take him into their confidence, if he would agree with their plans. What they would have done with him if he had not is, possibly fortunately, shrouded in mystery. Connolly's *Workers' Republic* newspaper had for some time been advocating insurrection, a dangerous development which might raise suspicions with the authorities.

Kathleen Clarke's account gives rather a different slant, insisting that Connolly had himself gone into hiding, giving instructions to his Citizen Army that if he was missing for four days they were to embark on rebellion. She quotes dialogue between MacDiarmada and Clarke, indicating that neither of them knew where Connolly was, and were annoyed by what they saw as playacting. However, she admits that some members of the Military Council might have acted without the full sanction of the council.[13]

Éamonn Dore, MacDiarmada's bodyguard, states that Ned Daly was instructed to wait with Dore and Frank Daly at the office of Séamus O'Connor, solicitor, in Dame Street, to be ready to take Connolly if he would not meet the IRB willingly. After a while, Ned went to see what was happening, and came back to say they could go home – Connolly had gone of his own accord.[14] If this story were true, Ned would surely have kept his brother-in-law informed of the event.

Joseph Mary Plunkett, of the Military Council, says that Connolly was 'invited' to a house in Dolphin's Barn, and finally agreed to go. He spent three days in discussions with Pearse, Plunkett and MacDiarmada, and was informed of all the plans and preparations. They convinced him that a rising was definitely going to happen, quite soon. From February, Connolly began to attend meetings of the Military Council, and became quite close to Plunkett. He gradually toned down the language used in his newspaper, but he had clearly been afraid that the war might end without Ireland having struck a blow, and that time was of the essence. Once assured that definite plans were in train, he appeared satisfied. Connolly himself never again alluded to this disappearance, even to his family.

Also in January 1916, there was a rumour that the authorities were preparing to swoop on the Volunteers and arrest the leadership. Edward Daly was sent for by HQ, and informed that the Volunteers were to stand to arms all night. However, no arrests took place.[15] The Rising was now definitely being planned for Easter, but hardly anyone but the Military Council was aware of this as yet.[16] The RIC and the Dublin Castle spies were suspicious, but could not find anything definite to work on.

The RIC was getting anxious:

> It [the Volunteers] is well organised, governed by a thoroughly disloyal directorate, and in the way of injuring recruiting and spreading sedition, does a great deal of harm ... It is probable that a great many of the IV merely joined in order to avoid military service, but the leaders, and many others, bitterly hate British Rule and would

no doubt do anything to weaken and embarrass England in the present struggle, if they thought it would serve their purpose.[17]

No one in the Dublin Castle administration seemed to be listening.

At a meeting of the Volunteer executive in February 1916, Pearse denied absolutely to MacNeill that a rebellion was being planned. However, both Pearse and Connolly had become convinced that only such an insurrection would save Ireland's soul. Pearse asserted, 'There are many things more horrible than bloodshed, and slavery is one of them.' Knowing that they were completely outgunned, the IRB were counting on German help, and the German General Staff had agreed to send 20,000 rifles to land in County Kerry in April. This would level the ground somewhat.

Darrell Figgis, a writer of republican sympathies who had purchased the German arms landed at Howth and Kilcoole in 1914, went to Limerick in February 1916, to deliver a talk on the financial pressures which British war taxation was imposing on Ireland. He visited the Daly home, and someone remarked that the family had not been at his lecture. 'One of the daughters of the house asked what was the good, since Ireland would be an independent Republic in less than three months, and would then be able to make her own financial provisions. This was said casually and coolly, as though one were informed that the next day might prove wet.' Figgis was astounded by this calm certainty – 'no wonder that my laboured lecture should seem nonsensical.'[18]

Training of the Volunteers continued. Bombs were constructed with tin cans. Volunteer Fergus de Burca recalled, 'We had soon used up all the empty tins that had accumulated over a long period [in St Enda's] ... I remember being sent by P H Pearse over to Tom Clarke's house in Fairview, to collect a case full which Mrs Clarke had in readiness.'[19] Seán Kennedy of C Company remembers intense routine training, 'arms drill, route marching and field exercise, in addition to my duties as an armourer undergoing training at the HQ of the Volunteers in Dawson Street ... Immediately prior to the rising, we were engaged in training in methods of street fighting which were conducted by Captain Robert Monteith, the area covered being Stoneybatter, Smithfield, Arbour Hill, Prussia Street, Aughrim Street and the surrounding district.'[20]

Arms and ammunition were being moved from place to place, and Peter Reynolds, a despatch rider, had a narrow escape in February when his motorcycle sidecar was searched by an RIC inspector. He had his baby daughter in the car, and the inspector said:

'I see she has some hardware under her,' seeing a biscuit tin full of revolvers and ammunition, and another box under the sidecar.

I remarked in a very shaky voice, 'Inspector, we are being watched; if two men want to live, you go one way, I'll go another.'

'Look, Reynolds,' he said, 'I'm on your side, but don't tell anyone.'

I very much doubted him, but he went away.[21]

On 20 February 1916, Edward Daly and Piaras Béaslaí met Gerald Griffin at the Broadstone railway station. Griffin was assistant quartermaster of the First Battalion, a member of the IRB and an employee of the Great Western Railway Co., working at the Broadstone.

We did not then tell him of the plans [for a rising] but we asked him to show us over the station. Afterwards he brought us out to Liffey Junction, and explained about all the 'loop lines', connections, points and signal boxes and how they could all be put out of action.[22]

Michael O'Flanagan, section commander of C Company, was being kept busy. In March, he moved thirty tins of petrol from Parnell Square to Clarkes' house in Richmond Road, and in April collected a number of bayonets and boxes of explosives from Dorset Street, bringing them to his father's home in Moore Street.

As my father, who was engaged in the poultry business, had a large quantity of feathers stored in barrels, I dumped the bayonets and the boxes of munitions for safe keeping among the feathers.[23]

Volunteer activities became more blatant, as if they were deliberately trying to goad the authorities to action. Inspector General Chamberlain of the RIC did his best to rouse Dublin Castle:

If the speeches of IV leaders and articles in SF journals have any meaning at all it must be that the force is being organized with a view to insurrection ... I submit it is now time to seriously consider whether the organizers of the IV can be allowed with safety to continue their mischievous work, and whether this Force so hostile to British interests can be permitted to increase its strength and remain any longer in possession of arms without grave danger to the state.[24]

The DMP was also remaining alert:

'Chalk' [an intelligence agent] reports that the young men of the IV are very anxious to start 'business' at once, and they are being backed up strongly by Connolly and the Citizen Army, and things look as if they were coming to a crisis, as each man has been served out with a package of lint and surgical dressing etc., and a tin for food similar to that issued to Soldiers.[25]

The day following this report, St Patrick's Day, the Dublin Brigade, practically fully armed, uniformed and equipped, paraded through the city of Dublin and held part of Dame Street, from the City Hall to the Bank of Ireland, for over an hour, during which time no traffic was allowed to break the ranks of the Volunteers, Citizen Army and Cumann na mBan.[26]

On St Patrick's Eve, Edward Daly warned Volunteer Jerry Golden to miss the parade the following day, because Golden had just transported a quantity of guns to HQ and would be well-advised to keep out of sight for a while. Daly then became more confidential.

> He told me he was looking forward to the Day ... He was sure I would do my duty as a soldier of the Republic. This was the first mention I had heard from anyone about a Republic, and when I asked him what he meant by it, he replied that when the day and hour had been settled on which to strike the blow for Irish freedom, the Irish Republic would be proclaimed by the Provisional Government of the Republic. He went on to say that some leaders would fall, but others would continue the fight. His eyes appeared to shine, and I saw he was in dead earnest in every word he spoke.[27]

On the Monday before Easter, a document was made public which outlined drastic measures to be taken by the British authorities against all nationalist groups, not just the Volunteers. The authorities announced that it was a complete forgery, but Eoin MacNeill and Patrick Pearse were convinced by it. However, Bulmer Hobson and others doubted it from an early stage. Of course the authorities must have had lists of suspect places and people, but the way the whole document was expressed was intensely inflammatory. It was suspected at the time that this 'Castle Document' was forged by Joseph Plunkett, to raise the temperature and prepare people for armed defiance. This cannot be proved either way; perhaps Plunkett merely embroidered an existing and authentic document. Evidence given by Dublin Castle witnesses at the subsequent Royal Commission seemed to admit that such a plan did exist, in some form.

On Saturday 15 April, Denis McCullough, director of the IRB in Belfast, came down to Dublin from the north, to try to find out what was going on.

> Tom [Clarke] told me, on his solemn word, that he knew nothing whatever about the arrangements or plans, that all he knew was that he was to report to Captain Ned Daly (his brother-in-law) on Easter Sunday morning and carry on under him. I am convinced that Tom was telling me the truth … He knew that the Rising was for Easter Sunday morning, but that was the total extent of his knowledge. He told me that Sean McDermott had control of all matters connected with the Rising, together – I think he said – with Pearse and Connolly, and I must get any information I required from him.[28]

It is clear that Tom wanted to be regarded as simply a member of the IRB, to stand aside when military action began – but of course the IRB were behind every action of the Volunteers.

Cracks were appearing in the Volunteer leadership. At a Cumann na mBan concert on Palm Sunday, 16 April, Bulmer Hobson issued a warning about the use of physical force. He recommended the Volunteers to continue developing their organisation, so that they could take part in the ultimate Peace Conference which would take place after the war, but insisted that 'no man had the right to sacrifice others merely that he might make for himself a bloody niche in history.'[29] Hobson had for some time suspected that the Military Council was moving towards an uprising, and believed that most of the Volunteers would be opposed to it.

On Tuesday, 18 April, a meeting of the Military Council was held at the home of Jennie Wyse Power, first president of Cumann na mBan, and the Proclamation was signed. Thomas Clarke came home and told his wife that the Volunteers would go into action the following Sunday, Easter Sunday. Kathleen was surprised when Ned did not mention it to her, and complained to Tom that he seemed to be still ignorant of any plans, which was not fair. Tom was annoyed, since Pearse was supposed to have issued orders to all the commandants, and had a long talk with Ned. Kathleen could see that Ned had got a bit of a shock: 'even though he knew the Rising would take place some day, this was very short notice. After that, I saw Ned only a few times, once when he asked me to buy material and make six signalling flags, which I did.'[30]

Volunteer Gregory Murphy spent Holy Week with fellow Volunteers Gerry Houlihan, Con Colbert and Con Donovan clearing depots and distributing arms, ammunition and explosives, and recalled, 'Though I heard nothing definite there was a sort of general understanding that the mobilisation on Easter Sunday was for a fight that night.'[31]

On Spy Wednesday, 19 April, Connolly informed his Citizen Army officers that an insurrection would take place on Easter Sunday, and that a shipload of arms was expected from Germany. That night a meeting of the Volunteer Executive was held, at which Hobson overheard a conversation about the date of the Rising. Next morning Kathleen Clarke left for Limerick with messages for John Daly and the Limerick Battalion. She brought her sons with her; they were to be left in Limerick with their aunts. This would not have been necessarily safer for them than Dublin, since Limerick was also to rise, but she probably wanted to be free to help Tom during the coming days, without having to be responsible for her children as well. Kathleen also brought a verbal message from Tom to tell them that 'John MacNeill has agreed to sign the Proclamation and is quite enthusiastic'.[32]

It is likely that Kathleen carried to Limerick the following undated letter from Edward Daly to his mother, obviously written in haste, on three pages torn from a notebook:

Thursday

Dearest Mamma

Just a few lines by K. who is going down.

Things here are very tense, no-one knows what might happen. However theres not much cause for you to worry as if trouble starts I will not be just in the firing line – best of being a boss I suppose. Besides I will be wearing a new garment that will stop most things. I must stop here but I suppose it will be some weeks before I can write again, & now there are many things in my head which I cannot write, but Mamma Dear, I want to tell you how I know and appreciate how good you have always been to me & how good all the others have been.

Give my love to everyone

Good Bye, Mamma. Ned

On Holy Thursday Captain Jim O'Sullivan, who had been checking on Volunteer preparations in County Wexford, got a wire from Pearse to return to Dublin. When he reported to St Enda's, he was told that Edward Daly wanted him in town.

While I cannot remember what words he [Pearse] used, or that he said anything definite about the rising, he certainly left me under the impression that something serious was about to happen.

O'Sullivan and Daly (both with motor cycles) met at Tom Clarke's shop, and Jim acted as courier between the shop and Tom's home in Fairview, collecting a parcel with money and a letter. Ned Daly addressed the First Battalion some time that day, telling them they would soon be given an opportunity of putting their drill into practice. They were to parade on Easter Sunday with twenty-four hours' rations, and hold themselves in readiness for action.[33]

Later that night when it was dark, having had a meal, Daly brought me [O'Sullivan] up to Fleming's Hotel in Gardiner Place where we met Tom Clarke and gave him the parcel ... [Clarke] was in great spirits. As we were leaving Fleming's Hotel, Daly informed me that the officers were not to stay in their homes from then on. He and I returned to the Four Courts Hotel, where we stayed the night. I then knew the Rising was timed for Sunday.[34]

Meanwhile, Section Commander Michael O'Flanagan was at 41 Parnell Square, distributing equipment, arms and ammunition among C Company, with instructions to hold them in readiness for use on further orders.

In Limerick, Kathleen found the leaders of the Limerick Brigade unprepared, and slow to make decisions. She had to wait for a response to take back to Dublin, so she spent Good

Friday at her mother's house, helping Cumann na mBan members to make up first-aid kits.

> My sisters ... were in a wild, but suppressed, state of excitement and enthusiasm, and quite sure of success. It amazed them when they found I did not feel the same way.

As she admits in her autobiography:

> I saw the force that could be mobilised against our small strength, and my reason could not see how our small strength could defeat that. It seemed to me the odds were too great, and as far as I was concerned I could see my happiness at an end. I felt Tom would not come through, and I think he knew he would not, but neither of us would admit it.[35]

MacNeill was still uncertain. Piaras Béaslaí refers to an early countermanding order:

> On Good Friday morning Daly ... showed me an order signed by MacNeill as Chief of Staff calling off all the parades and military movements planned for Easter Sunday. I stared at this, and asked what we were to do. 'It's all right now,' said Ned. 'Pearse, McDonagh and MacDermott have been talking to MacNeill this morning, and he has agreed to everything,' and he proceeded to burn the countermanding order ... Ned Daly's statement surprised me even more than the document. What happened at the interview is known

to no living person, but the others seem to have gone away with the (mistaken) impression that he [MacNeill] would offer no further opposition to their designs. Daly probably got his information from Seán MacDiarmada.[36]

That Good Friday, Edward Daly and two other officers lunched at the Red Bank Restaurant, D'Olier Street. Diarmuid Lynch handed him a sketch plan showing the manholes in the Four Courts area, through which the telegraph and telephone wires could be put out of action. One of the First Battalion officers, Phil MacMahon, later wrote to Jim O'Sullivan:

> You will recollect that on Good Friday 1916 I was helping Sean MacDermott and Tom Clarke on staff work and while with them in Parnell Street yourself and Ned Daly came along and joined us. We went into John Healy's and had a parting one – Sean, Ned, you and myself – and after a while Tom Clarke came outside and sent us about our business.[37]

Ordinary Volunteers were in a state of heightened expectation, but with little to do, having merely been told to 'stand to'. Volunteer Seán Price of B Company recalled:

> Good Friday was given up to keeping in contact with each other. This was easy to do for outside religious service we had no means of disporting ourselves. Many Volunteers found the occasion a good one for looking over and cleaning their

rifles and revolvers and seeing that their equipment was in good serviceable order ... We were all eager for news. We had of late become addicted to the question 'Any news?'[38]

Rumours were widespread – what did the 'stand to' order mean? Were there really German submarines in the Irish Sea? And something seemed to have happened down in Kerry ...

Ned had a busy day, clarifying roles and activities. Laffan recalled:

His first remarks to me were 'Lieut. Laffan, you are on active service from now on, and I am making your house, 35 Primrose Avenue, a stores for the 1st Battalion. Your first job is to go to Joe McGuinness's in Upper Gardiner St and remove all first aid equipment to your home to be left till required.'[39]

Among other responsibilities, Daly was given the job of arranging the arrest of Bulmer Hobson. Hobson was called to a meeting that evening, and put under guard in a house in Cabra Park. 'As far as I know,' said Fionán Lynch, captain of F Company, 'all the men guarding Hobson at Mairtin Conlon's were drawn from F Company. I know I posted guards there personally on 3 or 4 occasions ... The job was wished on me by Sean MacDermott and very embarrassing it was, as Bulmer was the "centre" of our circle of the IRB.'[40]

The Military Council were apparently afraid that Hobson would continue to persuade MacNeill to countermand the

Rising, and thought it better to keep him out of the way. He was rather distressed, and had to be warned to keep quiet, but did not show animosity towards his captors.[41] Hobson was released on the evening of Easter Monday, after the Rising had begun.

On Easter Saturday, Jim O'Sullivan remembered:

> I was running around with Daly, all day, making contact with various people, to ensure a full turn-out for Easter Sunday. On Saturday night, we contacted Sean McDermott in Kissane's house, Hardwicke Street. Sean reiterated that the bridges would be blown up and barricades erected, and that he would see that I had 50 extra men. Daly and I then went to the Clarence Hotel where we stayed that night.

Laffan, who was later made captain, helped in the removal of an ammunition dump to the Battalion HQ in Blackhall Place, and an armed guard was placed over it. He removed all the ammunition and food stored at Éamon Morkan's house on Ellis's Quay to his own home, including tinned milk, coffee, tinned meat, Oxo cubes and cheese. 'It took me well into Sunday morning to complete this work as the only means of transport I had was an ass and cart; no carrier would undertake the job.'

Captain O'Flanagan and a group of trusted men spent the evening collecting cases of guns, ammunition and home-made bombs from Parnell Square, and delivering them to two cottages adjoining the Four Courts in Church Street.[42]

However, that same evening word arrived in Dublin that Roger Casement had been arrested in Kerry, and that the *Aud*, carrying the essential arms from Germany, had been scuttled before it could be captured. This was a crushing blow to any hopes of success, and MacNeill immediately decided that an uprising would be nothing but a hopeless waste of life and resources. On Easter Sunday morning, the day to which all the months of preparation had been leading, he published newspaper announcements cancelling all Volunteer activities for that day. The IRB leaders were aghast; all seemed lost. Tom Clarke continued to argue for the Rising to take place on the Sunday as agreed, but he was overruled by the other leaders, who felt that most Volunteers throughout the country would be confused and demoralised by MacNeill's countermanding order. They decided instead to move the date to Easter Monday, and get word to as many Volunteers as possible.

Jim O'Sullivan expresses the disarray that followed the countermand.

On Easter Sunday morning, we [Daly and O'Sullivan] left the Clarence Hotel to go to Mass, when we saw the *Independent* placard, stating that Volunteer manoeuvres were cancelled. This news threw us into such a state that I don't remember if we went to Mass at all afterwards. As we were walking along we met several Volunteers who wanted to know what to do and if the newspaper announcement was true. We told them to parade at Blackhall Place [Columcille Hall], as arranged, and that any further information we got would be given to them there. I cannot remember much of what happened immediately afterwards, but we must have got information from somewhere, as, having dismissed the parade at Blackhall Place, we reported to Liberty Hall. This must have been sometime after twelve noon ... there was a conference in progress in another room, at which Connolly and Clarke, among others, were present ...

While we were waiting, Madame Markievicz came into the room, with a small automatic in her hand, and asked in a peremptory tone if anyone there knew where Hobson was ... 'I want to shoot him.' No one knew where he was at the time, so she went out [Ned Daly obviously kept his own counsel on this].

Sean McDermott came out and spoke to Daly and myself. I believe it was he told us that action was postponed until the following day at the same time, and to get busy on mobilisation arrangements, which we proceeded to do at once. I slept at home that night at Arranmore Avenue, North Circular Road.

Patrick Kelly, first lieutenant of G Company, First Battalion, went looking for information:

I was told Commandant E. Daly was upstairs [in Company

HQ]. I found him seated in a room alone. I explained my errand and was advised that the parade was off for the present. He instructed me to go home, remain there till called.[43]

Daly gave the same advice to Nicholas Laffan, who recalled:

This did not satisfy many of us. We were all on tenterhooks going around to see if we could get further information as to where the mobilisation was to take place. We staged a mock courtmartial in the Columcille Hall to while away the time, remaining on till midnight, when we left for home.

Later that Sunday, Jim O'Sullivan and Ned Daly kept a dinner engagement with Éamon Morkan, quartermaster of the First Battalion, and his wife Phyllis, a member of Cumann na mBan. They had recently been married, and Phyllis recalled that this would be the first dinner party she had given as a bride. She wrote:

They all arrived some time in the late afternoon. The men … were all looking very worried and took little interest in the dinner we had prepared for them.

Michael Staines recalled it slightly differently:

I left [Blackhall Place] about 10pm with Ned Daly, Jim Sullivan, Éamon Duggan and Ned Morkan and went to Morkan's home. We had supper there and talked over matters. We intended to stay up all night.[44]

Morkan himself recalled:

> On Sunday Daly, Sullivan and Duggan lunched with me at
> my home.[45]

Confusion over events is hardly unusual when remembering a time of such heightened tension, but it does seem odd
that the Morkans would have made a dinner engagement for
a day when they all actually expected action to have begun.
Phyllis continued:

> The men departed early to attend a meeting – a special
> one – which had been called suddenly ... my husband did
> not return until about 5 o'clock next morning. Ned Daly
> had left a suitcase containing his uniform, and on Monday
> morning, about 8.30, he and Jim O'Sullivan arrived .... in
> about half an hour my husband, Ned and Jim left the house,
> all in uniform and fully armed .... Ned told me before he
> left I would be happier in the fight helping, and if there was
> going to be fighting, they would need all the women they
> could get.[46]

When Phyllis and Éamon had a son in October 1916, he
was christened Edward Daly Morkan.

Piaras Béaslaí had been looking after Tom Clarke:

> Seán MacDiarmada came to me and said quietly: 'We're
> calling off the present arrangements, but keep your men
> together and wait for further orders.' He then asked me

to go with Tom Clarke as a bodyguard to a house on the North side. I readily complied. It would never do if Tom were arrested. As we walked together, Tom lamented Mac-Neill's action. 'It's an unexpected blow,' he said. 'All our elaborate plans are spoiled by this. I feel like going away to a corner to cry.' From a man who was normally unemotional in manner these words were very striking.[47]

That evening the lord lieutenant, Lord Wimborne, wrote to his chief secretary, Augustine Birrell, then on holidays in London, urging instant arrests to follow the loss of Casement's German arms:

> Nathan [the under secretary] proposes, and I agree, that Liberty Hall, together with two other minor Sinn Féin arsenals – Larkfield, Kimmage, and the one in Father Mathew's Park – should be raided tonight.[48]

It was decided at a conference at the Viceregal Lodge to arrest from sixty to a hundred nationalist leaders, and disarm as many as possible of the Dublin Volunteers, but they would wait for Birrell's consent before doing so. One way or another, matters were clearly coming to a head.

Chapter Four

• • • • • • •

Easter Week 1916

The Clock Strikes

*The hour has come to strike a blow For Freedom and the
Right,
And proudly, gladly do I go To meet the coming fight
'The Young Volunteer', Brian na Banban (Brian O'Higgins)*

Around 11.45 on Easter Monday morning, 24 April, just
as James Connolly was ordering the Volunteers and the
ICA to charge into the GPO, Commandant Edward Daly, his
eyes bright, stood before five companies of the First Battalion
at 5 Blackhall Place, and made the following announcement:

> Men of the First Battalion, I want you to listen to me for
> a few minutes, and no applause must follow my statement.
> Today at noon, an Irish Republic will be declared, and the
> Flag of the Republic hoisted. I look to every man to do
> his duty, with courage and discipline. The Irish Volunteers
> are now the Irish Republican Army. Communications with
> other posts in the city may be precarious, and in less than

an hour we may be in action.[1]

Battalion Adjutant Éamon Duggan's version is rather more succinct:

> I have an announcement to make. I wish you to receive it in silence. You are going into action in five minutes.[2]

This was a complete surprise to many of the Volunteers, who were scarcely prepared to put their lives on the line, starting *now*. Daly went on:

> We are going to fight the greatest power on earth and, let the battle be short or long, fight a clean fight, no brutality and don't stain the flag of Ireland.[3]

Some accounts say that he then read out the text of the Proclamation of Independence, and a history of A Company, First Battalion, records that he informed them they were now members of the Irish Republican Army, not the Irish Volunteers.[4] He indicated that those who had families or otherwise felt unable to take part could leave without reproach, and several did. Captain Alright, O/C G Company, was one of those who left, and Nicholas Laffan was promoted to his position. Another Volunteer started to leave, saying 'It wasn't for this I joined,' and Daly said quietly, 'We two will meet again.'

Most of the battalion members present were wildly excited, thrilled that their intensive preparations were

actually leading to a definite event. Ammunition and equipment were distributed, along with rifles of various denomi-
nations and calibres. 'What a miscellaneous selection of
material was "on parade" that morning, and the human element of a mixed brand too,' commented Seán Prendergast,
captain of C Company.[5] Their officers gazed with dismay on
the small turnout; estimates range from 120 to 150, and Jim
O'Sullivan initially put it at about 80 – out of a full strength
of 380.

The 'mobilisers' for each company had been out since
early morning, collecting as many men as possible. Seán
O'Duffy of A Company recalled, 'Just as I was going out the
back door in full equipment my mother gave me a dash of
Holy Water and I told her not to drown me.'[6] But there were
large gaps in the ranks; many Volunteers must have decided
that they were not ready for this adventure, and others had
simply been completely confused by MacNeill's countermand. Since all the battle plans had been predicated on full
battalion strength, serious changes were going to have to be
made. To start with, however, once all the arms had been
distributed, the various companies, some with only half-a-
dozen men, moved out from Blackhall Place to their planned
objectives.

Daly himself, having risen early and collected his uniform
from the Morkans' home with Jim O'Sullivan, had knocked
up the dispatch rider Peter Reynolds at 7.30am, saying 'Get

your clothes on quickly and come over to the drill hall.' Reynolds was in such a hurry that he forgot his revolver and ammunition, and had to dart back later, almost being caught by an RIC inspector. He asked Daly where they were going, and got the reply, 'We are going on a long journey and we may never come back.'[7]

It is likely that Reynolds was woken later than he recalled, because Michael O'Flanagan, section commander of C Company, said he himself was woken at 5.30am by Seán MacEntee, who had come down from the north. MacEntee needed to speak to GHQ urgently, so O'Flanagan took him to Clarke's home in Richmond Road where Daly was staying. He said that Clarke and Daly, in their pyjamas, interviewed Mac-Entee at about 7.45am, and MacEntee and O'Flanagan then headed to Liberty Hall. Phyllis Morkan said that Daly collected his uniform from her home at 8.30. One way or another, Edward Daly obviously had a busy early morning.[8]

There is a great deal of material available in the witness statements relating to the First Battalion in Easter Week, but people were remembering events thirty years in the past, so some contradiction is inevitable. The course of the Easter Rising itself was extremely confused and confusing, even at the time, and a coherent narrative is difficult to achieve. However, a clear picture can eventually be formed, and all historians of this period are indebted to the Bureau of Military History for collecting these witness statements.

The First Battalion had been designated to hold an area running from the Mendicity Institute on the south bank of the Liffey, through the Four Courts and on to Cabra, where they would link up with Thomas Ashe's company from the Fifth Battalion. The North Dublin Union was to be Battalion Headquarters. This whole area turned out to be the most strategically vital of the Rising, and Daly himself ultimately emerged as 'perhaps the shrewdest tactician among the rebel commandants'.[9]

There are well-established principles of military defence, particularly in regard to guerrilla warfare, as this fight was going to be. You need to have several lines of defence, one within another; you need to be aware of all possible directions of attack; all elements of your forces should be able to come to the aid of one another, or provide supporting fire. Additionally, the successful commander needs to provide for clear lines of communication with HQ, the possibility of reinforcement, regular food supplies, and the care of casualties.[10]

Joseph Plunkett, the IRB member who was responsible for the military planning, and was the Volunteers' Directory of Military Operations, had studied British military manuals in detail. He believed that the authorities would expect a rebellion of 'ten bloody fools in a field surrounded by rifles', and that the rebels would then take to the hills. He decided to take a defensive approach, which would put the aggressor at a disadvantage, and he correctly judged where reinforcements would be brought in, and could be stopped.[11] What went wrong with this plan was the lack of manpower, but there also seems to have been a certain shortsightedness in keeping the Volunteers holed up in numerous separate buildings, waiting to be bombarded out of them. The plan took for granted, of course, that the rest of the country would rise, and that the British troops in Dublin would be gradually surrounded by Irish Volunteers from other areas, possibly with German support.

Looking at his greatly depleted troops, Edward Daly realised that he could not stretch his lines of defence as far as originally planned, and that he would have to choose a more secure headquarters. The North Dublin Union would be too far from GHQ (the General Post Office in O'Connell Street) and could easily be cut off. His command area included a number of British army barracks, each of which would have to be either attacked or isolated. He rapidly decided to make the Father Mathew Hall, Church Street, his main headquarters. John Shouldice, lieutenant of F Company, contends that the convent of the French Sisters of Charity in Church Street was the HQ, not the Hall, but quartermaster Morkan makes clear that the convent was used for Monday night only, before the whole HQ staff moved to the Father Mathew Hall. Daly did not want to put the nuns at risk. The inner defensive area would consist of the Father Mathew Hall and the Four Courts. Barricades would be erected at the outer defences, to make access as difficult as possible.

As Ned Daly was making his announcement at 11.45, D Company of the First Battalion was already approaching the Mendicity Institute, under the leadership of Seán Heuston. They had been instructed by James Connolly to hold the building in order to attack any troops that might move down the quays from the Royal Barracks. This was intended to buy time for Daly and his men to complete their occupation of the Four Courts. Initially they were supposed to occupy the Mendicity for a few hours; once Daly's preparations were complete, Heuston was to withdraw. As it happened he decided to stay in the building. The British largely bypassed the Mendicity, and the fighting that took place around it was sporadic and brief, but intense. The building was captured quickly and with relative ease on Wednesday, as the British began to crush the Rising in earnest. While they were in the building, Heuston and his men had virtually no contact with Daly, as they looked rather to Connolly for instructions and reinforcements.

Another group of the First Battalion, a Special Forces unit, started the day by playing football with members of the Fianna outside the Magazine Fort in the Phoenix Park, the British army's central munitions store. This was a diversion; they suddenly mounted an attack on the Fort, with the intention of blowing it up. Some explosions and fires were achieved, but unfortunately for the plan, the main explosives store was left intact. One of the youngest casualties of the Rising occurred here, a lad of fourteen named Playfair, a son of the Fort's caretaker. Running for the nearest barracks to raise the alarm, he was shot in the back, having ignored a warning.

An inner line of defence, the Four Courts, the centre of Ireland's legal system, was quickly taken over by a section of C Company. The only resistance came from the policeman at the gate, who was taken prisoner. 'Every window was well barred with law books, and there are few better things for resisting a bullet than a row of books.'[12] Many of the prisoners taken during the week were kept in the holding cells of the Four Courts.

Outer lines of defence were erected around the North Dublin Union, Constitution Hill, Mary's Lane, North King Street and North Brunswick Street. Under the supervision of Ned Daly, barricades were constructed of anything that could be brought out from the surrounding buildings or found on the street – barrels, tables, sofas, carts, barbed wire, bricks from a building site. Local businesses, including a foundry, a builder's yard and a coach factory, were raided for materials, and broken glass was scattered around some of the barricades to delay cavalry approaches. These barricades proved extremely effective in an area which largely consisted of small passages and alleys, and was more like a rabbit warren than a battlefield. Paddy Holahan of the Fianna recalled one

barricade which had a cab in the centre: 'It was most con-
venient when you wanted to get through, as all you had to
do was open the door.'[13]

Volunteers Johnny O'Connor and Tom Sheerin, according to a 1966 radio interview, were among about sixty men
to hold North King Street, when there should have been at
least twice that number. Most of the men had Lee Enfield
rifles, with a few shotguns and a number of revolvers. A
small number had the Howth rifles, German Mausers, which
proved very unsatisfactory. Sheerin is clear that they had not
been told about the failure of the arms landing in Tralee: 'We
were led to believe that it had landed successfully ... I suppose that was to keep our hearts up.' Their morale was high,
because they were convinced that the rest of the country
would rise, particularly Cork and Limerick, which had well-
equipped brigades.[14] A notable feature of the First Battalion
defence was the number of excellent snipers in its ranks, and
these played an important part in the long week ahead.

One group of C Company, under Peadar Clancy, took
charge of Church Street Bridge. Seán Prendergast, in a group
under sergeant Mark Wilson, occupied a position from the
corner of Hammond Lane to Sharkey's Iron Foundry, commanding Chancery Lane. Here a policeman tried to cross
through the lines, and refused to halt or surrender. He was
overpowered, and received a revolver shot in the elbow, but
was heard to say, 'I'm as good an Irishman as any of ye.' 'We

admired his pluck but not his indiscretion,' said Prendergast, 'because a good deal of valuable time was wasted in dealing with him.'

The men had difficulty strengthening their barricades, as a number of 'separation women' – the wives of soldiers in the British army – kept trying to pull the structures down. Seán Kennedy was badly scratched on the face.[15] These women, not surprisingly, were very aggressive with the Volunteers, seeing them as traitors in time of war, and shirkers who ought to be in France themselves. Liam Archer of F Company, proceeding down Mary's Lane with fixed bayonet, was confronted by a large woman in a spotless white apron and shawl. 'Beating her ample bosom with clenched fists [she] called on me to "put it through me now for me son who's out in France". We steered past her ...'

Frank Shouldice, first lieutenant of F Company, was in charge of defending Church Street. His job was to keep the crossing between Church Street and North King Street open for his comrades, and to maintain communications with GHQ at the GPO. Commandant Daly later placed a barrel of sand at this crossing, and fixed a captured lance carrying a tricolour in it. Lieutenant O'Hegarty, erecting a barricade outside the Franciscan church in Church Street, was concerned that a passage led through the church grounds from Bow Lane, and decided to block it with seats from the church. Liam Archer recalled: 'A couple of the friars became very perturbed at this but the Superior drew them away, saying it was better they should be ignorant of what we did.'[16] In the end, the benches were left in the church.

Reilly's pub in Church Street, a corner site, became known as 'Reilly's Fort', and was fortified and filled with sacks of flour and meal taken from Blanchardstown Mills, on the opposite corner. It served as a shelter for F Company men on the barricades whenever they were relieved for rest periods. Holes were bored through the house walls with crowbars, and the company could thus reach North King Street and North Brunswick Street. Shouldice had about twenty men, a dozen rifles, six Howth rifles (which had limited ammunition supplies), six bayonets and a handful of revolvers. He requisitioned food supplies in the name of the Irish Republic from the nearby shops, and they cooked in Reilly's fireplace – stew, rashers, eggs and tea.

A house on the diagonal corner from Reilly's Fort commanded the North King Street – Smithfield side, and later came under heavy fire from snipers and armoured cars. Cottages backing on to Jameson's Malt House Granary were manned by Shouldice's company, and the Malt House Tower was used as a sniping post. Liam Archer found the Counting House: 'in a kitchen I found a bowl of stewed figs which I promptly ate – they were delicious, and with a couple of mugs of strong tea and some very fresh bread I had no other food for the week.'[17]

Employees of Jameson's were allowed in every morning and evening to turn over the barley in the Maltings, to prevent it going bad. Johnny O'Connor, in another radio interview broadcast in 1966, recalled how they warmly welcomed an old man who normally looked after Jameson's horses, because no one had any idea how to feed them, but they felt that barley might not be the right food for horses.

O'Connor admits that there was (naturally) 'any amount of whiskey' in the place, but insists that they were all too young to have a taste for it. Some small sample bottles were sent round to the barricades and to HQ in the Father Mathew Hall. However, they definitely helped themselves to Mr Jameson's best Havana cigars, and again sent a box to every barricade and to HQ.

O'Connor recalled two male civilians who offered to help them build barricades, but after a short time managed to tap a barrel in the yard and drink the whiskey out of billy cans. 'We had to cart them up to the Richmond Hospital. They'd taken too much of the stuff so that frightened everybody off.' Andrew Jameson apparently wrote an article after the Rising, praising the occupiers of the distillery for having done so little damage, although they had had enough whiskey under their control 'to set all Dublin mad'.[18]

The Ard Craobh (Central Branch) of Cumann na mBan had been told to meet in Mountjoy Square that morning, and await orders from Edward Daly. The message that finally reached them was that they should disband and go home. Self-described 'junior' member of the Cumann na mBan Leslie Price forgave this: 'You know the Volunteers, the kind of men they were; they thought that we should be away from all the danger'.[19] However, most of the women disobeyed the order, and some made their way immediately to the Father Mathew Hall, the other centre of defence. Phyllis Morkan arrived with fifty rounds of revolver ammunition.

As well as being First Battalion HQ, the Hall acted as a lock-up for prisoners, and as a first-aid post, where about a dozen members of Cumann na mBan looked after the wounded throughout the week. Tensions inevitably developed later, under the strain of prolonged anxiety, and it was alleged that some Volunteers were not taking their fair share of duty at the barricades, preferring to remain with the Cumann na mBan. In response to this, a young man named Howard left the hall to man one of the barricades, and was killed a short time later.[20]

Cumann na mBan members, including Jim O'Sullivan's sisters, Dolly and Mollie, were finally also permitted into the Four Courts. They were kept in a kitchen in the rear, cooking and washing up, and some of them left in disgust at not being allowed more active duties. There were good supplies of fresh meat, but the food otherwise was tinned. At night the women could luxuriate in the judges' ermine and sable robes, which provided very comfortable beds.

The Volunteers stripped the Battalion area of any supplies that could be gathered: weapons from a gunsmith, provisions from hotels and shops. According to most accounts, food was not a problem during the week; the Master of the North Dublin Union provided 10-gallon cans of soup nightly, and the nuns from St John's distributed meals.[21] However, Liam Archer later complained that food arrived in Church Street only in fits and starts, and other Volunteers seem to have seen little food during the week.

Casualty levels were low, so the women needed to do only first aid; local hospitals, particularly the Richmond, took in any seriously injured men. The Volunteers had initially tried to take this hospital over, but the staff refused to allow them to do so. However, the students and doctors worked continuously to help the wounded, providing first aid and stretchers. Blankets came from the residential quarters in Jameson's Distillery.

The earliest military casualties of Ned Daly's command, on Easter Monday, were part of a body of mounted Lancers, passing along the quays with ammunition wagons. First Lieutenant Patrick Kelly of G Company was arguing with a British soldier who was insisting on his right to go down North Brunswick Street. A number of local women joined in, urging the soldier to take Kelly's rifle. Suddenly, Kelly saw a mounted Lancer and a riderless horse coming up Church

113

Street towards him. 'I was about to press my trigger when I was commanded to stand steady. I became immovable and Comdt. E. Daly placed a .45 revolver on my shoulder, took steady aim and fired. The Lancer fell from the horse mortally wounded.'[22]

Edward Daly made a deliberate decision here, because others were quite ready to shoot this unfortunate Lancer. He may have needed to prove to himself that he could do it, since he had never shot anyone before. He probably also wanted to show his men that although he was younger than many of them, he was well able to lead them, and would not panic in the field. Laffan asserts that Daly merely hit the Lancer in the leg, and that he was subsequently brought to the Richmond Hospital.[23]

Some of the Lancers took cover in the Medical Mission and Collier's Dispensary on Charles Street. They were trapped there, but were able to unload the ammunition wagon carts they had been escorting, so could maintain fire. They later had to shoot some of their horses, who were maddened with hunger. Other loose horses galloped around the streets for hours. A number of Lancers were taken as prisoners to the Father Mathew Hall, and their horses were led to Sammon's Horse Repository in North King Street.[24]

On Monday evening, a postman was taken prisoner; his mail was seized, and sent on to the GPO. Commandant Daly remarked to Laffan that it was the first delivery of mails under the Irish Republic. Shouldice's Company had a very busy time on Monday evening and night with returning race-goers and holiday makers who were unable to travel via the quays to O'Connell Bridge. They were mostly in a state of panic, he said, and some were inclined to be obstreperous at being held up, wanting to know what it was all about.

That Monday evening, Ned Daly inspected the positions and gave the men the password for the night, 'Limerick'.[25] From that night on, other Volunteers began to arrive, and the battalion was almost up to full strength, about three hundred men, by the end of the week. But the British response was also under way; a brigade had arrived in Dublin from the Curragh Camp in Kildare, and was taking up positions at the Custom House, Amiens Street (now Connolly) Station and Dublin Castle. In England the 59th North Midlands Division, which consisted of regiments in training, was ordered to get ready for active service overseas. The men assumed, of course, that they were being sent to France, but found themselves in Dublin late on Tuesday evening.

On the outlying margins of the First Battalion area, Captain Jim O'Sullivan, with fifteen men of B Company, had headed towards the railway bridges at the North Circular Road and the Cabra Road, to prevent British troops approaching from that direction by damaging the railway lines. Jerry Golden of B Company gives a detailed description of events.[26] Heading up Constitution Hill, they were targeted by 'separation women' with rotten fruit and vegetables, but refrained from any response. At St Peter's Church, Phibsboro, O'Sullivan sent half of his group to take over houses on the Cabra Road, and led the rest up the North Circular Road. Earlier that Monday morning, O'Sullivan had caught sight of the Dublin Corporation employee who was supposed to have demolished the railway bridges, and was surprised he was still in the city; he should have been doing his demolition work. On arrival at the North Circular Road bridge, they found no barricades had been erected as planned, and the bridge was still intact. O'Sullivan's men were not properly equipped to complete this task, as it had not been part of their responsibilities.

They began to erect barricades, then observed a party of about two hundred mounted Lancers, escorting a cart, coming towards them. O'Sullivan ordered his men to take cover in the garden of St Peter's presbytery, and let the Lancers pass towards the quays. All the crossings leading to the city were meant to be under Volunteer control by this time, and O'Sullivan assumed that the Lancers would not get much further. He had too few men to attack such a large group, and his ammunition supplies were low. He also expected that more British troops would be arriving later, and that he should hold his ammunition supplies in reserve. 'Some of the men grumbled about this decision at the time,' he wrote later, 'but I thought it was the best thing to do at the moment.'[27]

The arrival of the Lancers further along, at the North Circular Road, caused some amazement there, where a small group under Francis Daly, O/C Engineers, had been trying to blow up Connaught Street bridge. They had expected that O'Sullivan's men would prevent any British force coming near them. The Lancers opened fire on them, and they decided to concentrate on destroying the railway line, since they did not have enough explosive to destroy the bridge. They cut the rails at intervals, continually under fire, and finally found themselves out at Ashtown, where they helped to demolish telephone wires. They made their way back to the Four Courts by the afternoon, and helped with building the barricades.

From the early evening, O'Sullivan's men prevented returning race-goers from going along the main road, and made them go through Connaught Street and Fassaugh Lane. They did not want anyone to be able to report how few they were. They spent the night in nearby houses, and at 5am on Tuesday Seán Howard, one of the youngest of the Volunteers, began to try to make a hole in the tram sets to insert explosives. The only tools he had were a cobbler's hammer and a coal chisel. When a sufficient depth was finally achieved, the first lot of explosives did not work, because the men attempting the job, being inexperienced with explosives, had not realised they needed detonators. Jim O'Sullivan was able to provide these, but of the wrong size, so two of the men crimped them in with their teeth, and a certain amount of damage was eventually achieved.

Shortly, however, it became clear that the British had set up machine guns at Great Western Square, Broadstone Station (the former Dublin terminus of the Midland Great Western Railway), and Upper Grangegorman, and O'Sullivan's group came under heavy fire. His position was no longer tenable, and he decided to withdraw towards the Four Courts area. Two of his men instead joined the remainder of B Company, on the Cabra Road, and subsequently headed south to try and find the Fifth (Fingal) Battalion. O'Sullivan found it impossible to make his way back to Battalion HQ, and eventually ended up in the GPO, where he later took part in the 'O'Rahilly Charge' and the retreat along Moore Street. He did not see his close friend Daly again until they were held under arrest in the Rotunda Gardens.

Later, talking to Thomas Ashe when they were interned in Frongoch Camp, O'Sullivan found that Ashe had expected him to fall back towards the Cabra area, rather than towards the city, as O'Sullivan had understood.[28] The First Battalion area adjoined that of the Fifth Battalion under Ashe, in that area, and the two battalions were supposed to remain in communication. Ashe had left a Volunteer at Cross Guns Bridge to receive any messages from Ned Daly, but none ever arrived. Béaslaí's memoir says that Daly never mentioned this to him, although they had gone over all the plans in minutest detail. Either Daly forgot about the arrangement, or a message miscarried. It was one of the numerous 'mix-ups' of the week, Béaslaí ruefully added.[29]

The Broadstone railway station, which was to form part of the outer defences, was not attacked by A Company on the Monday as planned. This was a major strategic error, because the Broadstone commanded a good view of the Battalion area, looking down Constitution Hill, and had been central to the original plans in terms of disrupting rail transport. Because the company was well under strength on Monday, Captain Denis O'Callaghan decided they were undermanned for such an attack. A Company instead occupied some houses on North King Street, and erected barricades.

Daly insisted that they try to approach the station again on Tuesday, but by then a unit of Dublin Fusiliers had taken it over. The Volunteers were fired on, and driven back to North Brunswick Street. Here Clarke's dairy and provision shop, a four-storey building, provided a good vantage point for Volunteer snipers. Company HQ was Moore's coach-works. Daly instructed them to keep the station under fire, to prevent an attack from it. However, Broadstone was lost; if the railway bridges were to be captured from the Volunteers, British troops would now be able to get into central Dublin by rail.

Ned Daly's battalion area, although it contained the massive structures of the Four Courts and several British army barracks, was also a place of small streets and lanes containing pubs, shops and crowded tenement houses.

In Dublin at that time, around sixty thousand people lived in slums and tenements; many of the city councillors were slum landlords, with no interest in improving the city's housing. Life in the poverty-stricken tenements was a day-to-day struggle against hunger and disease. The Easter Rising burst on this oppressed population like a thunderbolt, rendering already insecure lives even more uncertain. Some of the worst slums were in the Four Courts area. Church Street in particular was heavily overcrowded; its 181 houses contained about 2,000 people.[30]

The First Battalion tried to avoid civilian casualties, and they did their best through that week to maintain food supplies for people who could no longer reach local shops because of heavy fire. The battalion area included Monks's Bakery in North Brunswick Street, and this was kept working throughout the week, providing bread for anyone who could reach it. It was held by G Company under Captain Laffan, and the Monks family was impressed by the discipline of the men, and by the fact that money was provided by Ned Daly to pay for the bread used.[31] Bread was sent to the convent in North Brunswick Street, and the nuns sent back hot soup in return.

Despite efforts at reassurance, people began to leave the city. Some Volunteers, racing to join the Rebellion and arriving late on Monday evening, 'met every conceivable description of vehicle coming out – motor-cars, brakes, cabs, jaunting-cars, carts, hand-carts, bicycles, perambulators. They were all packed with refugees or their belongings.'[32] However, many families decided to stay where they were; they had nowhere to go, and were afraid to leave their homes undefended.

Francis Daly, O/C Engineers of the First Battalion, having got back from Ashtown to the Four Courts, headed out with Christy McEvoy on the Monday night to cut the railway lines at Blanchardstown with explosives, but they could not get back into the city and spent the night in Glasnevin Cemetery. When they finally returned, Daly instructed them to concentrate on damaging railway lines, but to use explosives on any British government property as well, such as barracks and post offices. They were able to collect gelignite from the GPO and made their way to the railway line at Clonsilla, narrowly escaping capture by a group of Lancers. One of these said, 'You have dropped one of your sugar sticks, sonny', as a stick of gelignite fell out of Christy's pocket, but Christy simply picked it up and put it back. They had little success trying to destroy the line, and ultimately ended up in County Meath, where they witnessed the Battle of Ashbourne.

Communications were maintained as well as possible. Cumann na mBan members were very active as couriers. Leslie Price and Brid Dixon travelled every evening between the GPO and the Father Mathew Hall.

> We used to have great gabbing and talking I needn't tell
> you with Ned Daly and with any of the men or Cumann
> na mBan who might be there and we would bring back the
> messages. I remember the second night we were going out
> Seán MacDiarmada gave us two officers' canes – they have
> steel tops to them. He said, 'If anyone touches you, use that
> on them.' [33]

The Fianna also fulfilled this dangerous task. Joseph
Reynolds, aged sixteen, spent the week acting as courier
between Daly's HQ and the GPO, and scouting for signs of
British troops and barricades. Movement became more and
more difficult as the British cordon tightened, and he spent
the latter part of the week in shelter with the Capuchin
fathers, until the surrender had been completed. [34]

Ignatius Callender, a section leader of D Company, went
backwards and forwards to the GPO on a bicycle, and it was
on one of these occasions that he heard that thousands of
Germans had landed at Kerry and were marching on Dublin;
this news temporarily delighted the men on the Church
Street barricades. Callender had 110 rounds of .303 ammunition in his home, and offered to bring it to Church Street.
However, his mother, observing what he was doing, insisted
on taking it herself. She put it inside her blouse and went off
with a milk jug, pretending she was getting milk. A British

officer questioned her, but another officer nearby knew her by name, and she was let through. She delivered the ammunition to the house of the Murnane family in Blackhall Place, and Mrs Murnane brought it to the barricades. Daly later sent thanks to the ladies involved.[35]

Liam Archer of F Company, in Church Street, was concerned about discipline. Men would wander away from their posts, looking for their pals or for food, as food supplies were intermittent.

> This was particularly bad at night, and called for frequent inspections ... In retrospect, I realise that we should have organised sentries' tours of duty, rest points, etc. But we were very ignorant.

This ignorance is surprising, considering the accounts of endless drill and lectures, and the detailed preparations, but some of the more experienced Volunteers may have been among those who did not turn up. Every Company started the week well below strength, and sometimes it was the officers who were missing.

By Wednesday, British army reinforcements were at full strength. Fire from machine-guns and artillery was incessant, and from the Liffey could be heard the boom of the armed naval vessel *Helga*, shelling the city centre. One of the Capuchin friars from Church Street, who supported the Rising, began hearing confessions in the convent, and was kept busy.

Patrick Kelly was one of those who took the opportunity:

> After hearing my Confession Fr. Albert addressed me as follows: 'Go forth now, my child, and if necessary die for Ireland as Christ died for mankind.' I felt exalted and could have faced the entire British army single-handed.[36]

Father Albert was not representative of all priests, of course – Joseph McDonough, at his barricade, was reviled by a curate from St Paul's, Arran Quay, condemned for rebelling against established authority, and informed that he would end up in hell.[37] Archer's men in Church Street were visited by two priests who, though annoyed with them, gave them conditional absolution.

It was on Wednesday that a crucial battle took place at Mount Street Bridge, on the Grand Canal. Volunteers occupied houses in Northumberland Road, overlooking the bridge, and two of the British army battalions which had just arrived from England marched into a trap. The intense fighting lasted for several hours, with the Volunteers eventually being driven from their positions. However, over two hundred British soldiers lay dead. The South Staffordshire regiment, which was later implicated in the deadly events in North King Street (see Chapter 5), witnessed this battle and its aftermath, and would have been fired up to take revenge on the Volunteers, or anyone else who got in their way.

By this time, an unwilling respect for the rebels was

beginning to be felt in the city. They had held on to their posts for much longer than anyone could have expected, even themselves. They were heartened by the rumours that German troops were landing: Eileen Murphy saw 'Ned Daly and Fionán Lynch studying the map, with particular attention to the Naas Road. There was terrible disappointment when nothing came of it.'[38] The mental and physical stresses were beginning to take their toll, and small comforts meant a lot. Eilís Ní Riain looked after Commandant Daly in the Father Mathew Hall.

> I remember taking off his boots and socks on Wednesday, bathing his feet and giving him fresh socks with plenty of boric powder. He said he felt very comfortable after it.[39]

At this stage, Ned was still unaware that the bridges had been lost, but he must have been wondering how his close friend O'Sullivan was getting on.

On Wednesday afternoon, a heavily-laden woman came to a barricade in North Brunswick Street, insisting that she was bringing back bread for her children. When the sentries pulled back her shawl, however, they found an array of silverware, teapots and coffeepots. Volunteer Patrick Kelly was at a loss what to do, so he allowed her to go on to Lisburn Street. By this stage looting was rife in the main shopping streets of the city, though highly dangerous because of sniper fire. Kelly was later disgusted to discover that another woman they had let through the barricades, of tall and muscular build, had been a British soldier in disguise – they had not got word of him in time.

On Wednesday, an attack was launched on the group of Lancers who had gone to ground in Charles Street. At least one Volunteer was wounded, and the Lancers managed to extinguish incendiary devices thrown through the window. The Volunteers rescued their wounded comrade, but were now coming under fire from British snipers, perched on the tower of Christ Church Cathedral, the tower of Powers distillery and the Bermingham tower of Dublin Castle.[40]

Later that Wednesday, Edward Daly had to turn his attention to the nearby Linen Hall Barracks, north of King Street. It overlooked the Battalion's area, and would be a constant danger if it was fortified by British troops. He sent A Company to attack it, and more than forty British army pay staff were taken prisoner. However, it was impossible to hold the barracks with the numbers available, so the building was set on fire to prevent reoccupation by the British army. The fire spread uncontrollably into Bolton Street, lighting up the sky and revealing defended positions.

Some tenement houses were at risk of destruction, but hoses were brought from the North Dublin Union and enough water was available to save them. The fire took Hugh Moore & Alexander's, a wholesale druggist, where there were large stores of oils and spirits; these exploded, sending flames hundreds of feet into the air. Daly had been contemplating an attack on British forces in Capel Street who were sniping at the barricades, but the brightness of the fires rendered this plan impossible. Besides, his men in this area were now exhausted from fighting the fire; they had also had to fight off some of the inhabitants of the houses, who had thought they were trying to burn them out.[41]

As a later commentator said, 'There is a good military lesson here: a defending force should never deliberately set off a fire in their area, for this is only helping the attacker.'[42] It is not clear whether Daly gave the order to start the fire, or if the men on the spot took the decision, but Julia Grenan, a member of Cumann na mBan who had been acting as courier, was told later that a dispatch she had been given in the GPO for Ned Daly had contained instructions to blow up the Linen Hall Barracks.[43]

The constant barrage of artillery, the noise and smoke of the raging fires all around, and the realisation that his options were continually narrowing, made Ned Daly's position in the Father Mathew Hall increasingly uncomfortable. He ordered the destruction of a footbridge across Bow Street, which was making the back of the Father Mathew Hall vulnerable to attack. By now, communication with the GPO had been almost completely cut off by a British advance from Dublin Castle via City Hall towards Capel Street, although Peter Reynolds was still making daring sorties on his motorbike.

Leslie Price gives a very vivid picture of a harassed Ned Daly, his uniform torn and dusty, his hands and face black with smoke, trying to deal with pressures from all sides.

There were three married women around Ned Daly, Mrs Martin Conlan, Mrs Frank Fahy and Eddie Morkan's wife. Their husbands were in the Four Courts. They were kind of pestering Ned Daly with questions as to how their husbands were.

Another officer described him as 'beginning to look very tired and haggard. His tunic was torn at the sleeve. I believe that he had not closed his eyes since the outbreak on Monday'.[44]

Immersed as he was in the heat of battle, Daly, who was fulfilling all the dreams of his unknown father and his indomitable uncle John, must have occasionally wondered what was happening back home, where his excited sisters had been so eagerly awaiting the start of the action. However, Limerick's story of the Easter Rising is one of uncertainty and confusion, leading to an ultimate failure to engage.

The Limerick Battalion planned to hold the line of the Shannon from the Clare side, and had expected to receive some of the arms arriving at Fenit, County Kerry, under Roger Casement's direction. Having mustered his troops at Killonan, just outside Limerick, Commandant Michael

L-r: Ned Daly, Gerald Griffin, Jim O'Sullivan.

Edward Daly's last letter to his mother.

Sheet 1:

No.   Date.   Time   Place

To   Place

Thursday

Dearest Mamma,
    Just a few line[s]
[C.] K. who is going
down.
    Things here a[re]
very tense, n[o one]
knows wha[t will]
happen. How[ever]
there's not much [use]
for you to worry [un]
til trouble starts

From

Sheet 2:

No.   Date.   Time   Place

To   Place   Place

will not be [just in]
the firing line — [bes]
of being a boss I
suppose. Beside[s]
I will be wearing
a new armen[t] that
will stop most thing[s]
but I must stop h[ere]
well suppose it
before I can writ[e]
again, & now there are

From

Sheet 3:

No.   Date.   Time   Place

To   Place

many things in my
head which I
cannot write, but
mamma dear, I want
to tell you [how]
I know & appreciate
how good you have
always been to me
& how good all the
others have been
Give my love to Everyone
Good Bye Mamma, [Ned]

From

Above and below: Four Courts.

Above: Linenhall Barracks.

Below: Richmond Barracks. **Opposite:** Damaged façade of Four Courts.

Items given by Ned
to his sisters the night
before his execution.

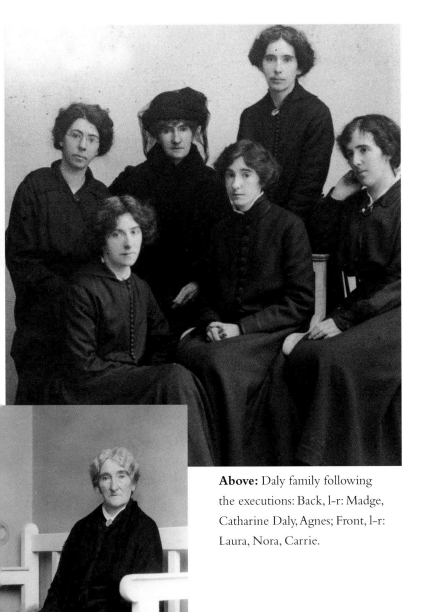

Above: Daly family following the executions: Back, l-r: Madge, Catharine Daly, Agnes; Front, l-r: Laura, Nora, Carrie.

Left: Catharine Daly in old age (late 1930s), in Tivoli.

Above: Catharine Daly's funeral, 1 May 1937.

THOUSANDS HONOR NED DALY'S MOTHER AT HER FUNERAL IN LIMERICK

Remains of Patriotic Irish-woman, Who Thanked God That Her Son Fought and Died for Ireland, Escorted to Grave by Cortege Two Miles in Length.

On April 23, at Tivoli, Limerick City, there passed away as noble-souled an Irishwoman as ever carried he cross for Ireland, Mrs. Catherine Daly,

Left: One of many newspaper articles covering Catharine Daly's death.

Colivet was to attack British positions in Limerick, cutting telephone wires and destroying railway connections. Another group was to take charge of west Limerick, and units would also be active in Tipperary and Clare. The aim was ultimately to send a train with the Fenit arms to Dublin, along with as many Volunteers as possible, as soon as the Limerick area was secure. On Easter Saturday, primed for action, almost three hundred Limerick Volunteers paraded past John Daly's home in Barrington Street, as the old man watched from his window.[45]

The O'Rahilly, director of arms on the Volunteer Executive, arrived at the Daly home on Easter Sunday morning with MacNeill's countermand message. Madge Daly refused to accept its authority, and was very severe with The O'Rahilly, as he told MacDiarmada when he got back to Dublin. John Daly had lost his voice, but Madge was undoubtedly expressing his sentiments also.[46] Colivet, however, did accept the authority of the message, and sent out orders to all the other units, cancelling the arrangements. He then marched the City Battalion to Killonan as if it was a routine bivouac, and there on Monday morning he got the news of the loss of the arms in Kerry. This was followed by the arrival at Killonan of two of the Daly sisters, Agnes and Laura, with a message which read:

> Dublin Brigade goes into action at noon today (Monday).
> Carry out your orders. (Signed) P.H. Pearse.

Colivet consulted with his officers. All their plans had been based on having the Kerry arms, and without them they felt there was no hope of success. They suspected that probably only a small number of Volunteers had gone into action in Dublin, along with the Citizen Army, and these could hardly hold out for long. Besides, all the outlying Limerick units had now been demobilised, and there were only about eighty men under arms at Killonan. Above all, MacNeill was chief-of-staff, and it was his order which should be obeyed. Taking all this into consideration, the unanimous decision was that nothing could be done.

The men were marched back to the city, and dispersed. Later the British officer commanding the district demanded the arms of the Limerick Battalion, and these were surrendered to Mayor James Quinn on Friday 5 May. Alphonsus O'Halloran accepts that Colivet could not be blamed for the failure to act, considering the degree of confusion, but he expresses annoyance that the rank and file were ignored when the decision was made, while non-combatant members of the Management Committee were allowed to vote.[47] The failure of the Limerick Volunteers, John Daly's protégés, to come out in Easter Week was greatly lamented by many of them, and created feelings of bitterness and dissension in the area for many years.

Volunteer Éamonn Dore, Seán MacDiarmada's body-guard, had gone home to Kerry for Easter. On getting word of the Rising, he caught a train from Limerick to Dublin on the Tuesday, travelling with Laura and Nora Daly. Kathleen Clarke said he met them by accident, recognising them because of their resemblance to their brother, but Milo McGarry, who had helped to bring the message from Pearse, said that he met Dore at the Dalys' home, and they all travelled together back to Dublin.[48]

The girls were hoping to find out what on earth was going on, and perhaps bring back fresh orders for the Limerick Volunteers. In Dublin, avoiding British patrols, they found their way to their sister Kathleen's home, where she gave them what news she had; she had been getting regular messages from the GPO. The gas had been cut off, so the girls and Dore had supper by candlelight, then set off to walk to the GPO. Kathleen wanted desperately to go with them, but knew she would not be able to walk that distance.

They reached the GPO after midnight, and were joyfully welcomed by Clarke and MacDiarmada. They were urged to get a message to Terence MacSwiney and Tomás MacCurtain in Cork; MacSwiney knew the Dalys well, and would trust them. The Cork Volunteers must cause a diversion in the south, and prevent the British troops from massing around Dublin. Dore says, 'The message to Limerick was less friendly when Seán MacDiarmada delivered it ... I would prefer not to give the exact wording.' MacDiarmada, turning to Dore, then said, 'Éamonn, you need not come back as you know it's all over.'

Back at Kathleen's house, the girls rested for a short while, then got the 6am train back to Limerick. Dore, having seen them off, managed to work his way back to the GPO, sustaining a slight leg wound. He was able to report that the British were in the Rotunda, Phibsboro and the corner of Parnell Street.

Meanwhile, the girls found that one section of the train was going to Cork. Nora managed to stay on it, pretending she had lost her ticket, and eventually contacted the Cork Volunteers. However, MacSwiney and MacCurtain told her it was impossible for them to do anything, as they were surrounded by British military. They would not take action unless they were attacked. Mary MacSwiney, Terence's sister, took her home for the night. Nora tried to get to Dublin in the morning, but found all trains were stopped, so headed back home.[49] The Cork Volunteers ultimately surrendered their arms.

So the Daly sisters arrived back in Limerick, separately, primed with accounts of the great deeds in Dublin, but probably fully aware that the end could not be far away, and that for them it would be tragic.

Chapter Five

27–29 April 1916

Journey's End

Thursday morning broke to the roar of flames, the unrelenting sound of machine-gun fire and the heavier boom of the British gunship *Helga*, which had begun to aim shells at the Four Courts. Edward Daly was still in the Father Mathew Hall, but he would soon have to move his HQ to a more defensible building. He and his officers were exhausted. All over the city, the positions held by the Volunteers were becoming untenable, communications were breaking down completely, and a heavy pall of smoke hung over the city centre.

Seán Prendergast, O/C C Company, recalled vividly the absolute exhaustion of the garrisons:

> The average among us had lost the sense of sleep ... Just
> a few times I had seen others while on duty at a window

'napping'. I myself fell victim; I was 'dead beat' and unable to keep my eyes open for any length of time. It might have lasted for seconds or minutes. When I came to I found myself standing at a window grasping a rifle ...[1]

C Company had captured the Bridewell police station, next to the Four Courts, on Monday; it provided useful cells for prisoners, as well as for the few policemen who had been taken with it. On Thursday, the company was ordered to evacuate it and go to Reilly's Fort instead, where they would be more useful. In his recollections Michael O'Flanagan continued:

> When we got as far as the Father Mathew Hall I met Commandant Ned Daly on the street ... He told me that he was short of men and that as he required an escort to take some enemy prisoners ... from the hall to the Four Courts, I was to divide my party, sending half of it as an escort with the prisoners, and the other half to Reilly's Fort ...We had some difficulty crossing North King Street as the fire from enemy forces located around the technical schools in Bolton Street was very intense.

When they arrived at Reilly's Fort, O'Flanagan argued with the post commander there, Lieutenant Maurice Collins, that the situation was very exposed, and that they would not be able to retreat safely from it. Collins emphasised that there was no intention of retreating – their job was to fight to a finish. O'Flanagan and his men were kept under constant fire over the next two days, as the British forces drew closer; the Volunteer ammunition supplies were dwindling.[2]

In the early hours of Thursday morning, Lieutenant Allen instructed members of C Company on the Four Courts' roof to fire six rounds each into the air. He emphasised that Howth rifles must be used – these had a very distinctive sound when fired. No reason was given for this order, but Seán Kennedy speculates that it was to draw enemy fire away from hard-pressed comrades elsewhere. 'I forgot that the Howth rifle, not being furnished with wooden casing, would be very hot after use and in grabbing it with my hands I got severely burned from the red-hot barrel.'[3] They came under intense fire from concealed snipers, and by mid-day were forced to withdraw to the first landing overlooking Hammond Lane, where Lieutenant Allen was mortally wounded by a sniper.

Liam O'Carroll, a lieutenant of A Company, spent part of Thursday in the Four Courts, escorting the Capuchin fathers Albert and Augustine, 'who interviewed every member of the garrison and attended to their spiritual wants'. It is symptomatic of the exhaustion they all suffered from that he added, 'I have no clear recollection as to the events of Friday or Saturday.'

Phyllis Morkan stayed at the Father Mathew Hall until Thursday. She then left with May Kavanagh, Éamon Duggan's fiancée, to look for supplies of brandy or whiskey (as stimulants for the hospital) and supplies of clean clothes, but she found her home in the possession of the British military, and was unable to return to the garrison.

George O'Flanagan of C Company spent Thursday with six other Volunteers, armed with Martini Henry rifles, sniping from the top windows of the Four Courts facing the quays. They had thirty rounds of ammunition each. British troops emerged from Essex Street, on the quay across the river, and started to fire at the Four Courts with a field gun, driving the snipers back. O'Flanagan spent Friday on top of a building with a good view of Church Street, and provided covering fire for the retreat of their comrades back down the street.[4] Joseph McDonough of C Company, at Church Street Bridge, was part of a group who took over the public house opposite Hand's, and set it on fire so it could not be used by the British. It went up in flames, along with a tram car which had been abandoned in front of the house.[5]

British armoured cars made their way to Charles Street on Thursday evening, and finally rescued the beleaguered Lancers from the Dispensary and the Medical Mission. Starving and exhausted as they were, they had fought off a determined Volunteer assault on Wednesday, extinguishing an incendiary advice that was thrown in a window and wounding Volunteer Paddy Daly. The improvised armoured cars backed up to the doors of the Medical Mission and the Lancers were able to move their wounded into the cars, along with the body of one of their officers, ducking a hail of sniper bullets as they did so. Their consignment of ammunition was also retrieved.

A British cordon was then erected from Bridgefoot Street and Queen Street, along North King Street, to Bolton Street and Capel Street. The Volunteers had assumed that the main attack would come from the west, but no troops advanced from the barracks there, or from Kingsbridge (now Heuston) Station. There was no frontal assault on the Four Courts, and the building was not bombarded again after the first artillery assault.

The Father Mathew Hall would now have to be abandoned as a headquarters, as it was becoming completely surrounded. Daly was still holding things together; Callender, section leader of D Company, describes him as 'at all times solicitous for each and every one of his men. He cared nothing for himself or any hardship he endured ... I will treasure his memory forever. Gentlemanly, courteous and brave.'[6]

The Four Courts became the final headquarters on Friday evening, as Commandant Daly decided that he should consolidate what strength he had left.

> He may have left this move dangerously late, since it was by then a daunting task to move his men back down Church Street – a task made more difficult and dangerous by Daly's own barricades ... Daly was effectively cut off from his men who held out in the shrinking King Street battleground.[7]

On his arrival at the Four Courts, Daly ordered that the

restaurant's stocks of alcohol should be poured into the sewers.[8] In fact, it was noted by Captain RK Brereton, one of the British army prisoners, that these supplies had been left untouched: 'there was no sign of drinking amongst them, and I was informed they were nearly all total abstainers.'[9]

A commentator on the Four Courts garrison later remarked:

> It is worthy of note, and reflects upon their Commander, that though much damage might have been done archives and documents, scarcely anything was touched.[10]

Dublin Castle had been concerned in this regard, as Viscount Wimborne wrote to General Maxwell on 29 April:

> The Lord Chancellor has left a plan here of the Four Courts showing the position of an isolated building containing all the most valuable and historical documents in Ireland and also, although less important, the secret position where the Great Seal was last deposited.[11]

By Friday, Jervis Street hospital contained about thirty bodies. As well as treating wounded Volunteers, the medical staff were also dealing with civilians who had been wounded while desperately searching for food, or had ignored the night-time curfew. Johnny O'Connor realised, looking at Jameson's Distillery beside his barricade, that the lights he thought he saw in its windows were actually reflections of the fires that were consuming O'Connell Street and beyond. It was clear to him that the end must be coming.[12]

James Connolly, in the GPO, was dictating a manifesto to his secretary, Winifred Carney. Addressed to the Volunteer forces in the field, it spoke in glowing terms of the progress they had made: 'For the first time in 700 years the flag of a free Ireland floats triumphantly in Dublin City.' The first command he mentioned was that of the First Battalion, under Edward Daly:

> Commandant Daly's splendid exploit in capturing Linen-hall Barracks we all know. You must know also that the whole population, both clergy and laity, of this district are united in his praises.[13]

Éamon Morkan moved the headquarters of his A Company to the Four Courts on Friday. Annie Fahy was there, helping with the cooking, and that day was able to milk a goat which had strayed into the green area of the Four Courts; she remembered with pleasure the change from endless condensed milk in the tea.[14] All that day Father Augustine again heard confessions, and the men were given permission to receive Communion in St John's convent, since they were now cut off from the chapel in Church Street. Nicholas Laffan had not had a shave or a wash for a week, and admits being ashamed of his dirty appearance in front of the nuns.

Laffan's group, from G Company, was manning barricades at Red Cow Lane, under constant fire from a British armoured car.

> When night fell [Friday] the firing became more intense from all sides. The enemy made a sudden attack from Lurgan and Coleraine Streets and from the Smithfield end. This was the worst night we had. With the glare of the fires it was hard to detect their movements, as they could attack, retire and then come in stronger numbers. I remember standing in a corner of Moore's Factory on Friday night and the rifle and machine-gun fire from the enemy was so intense that to cross the room was certain death.[15]

The guarding and feeding of prisoners (military, police, and civilians who got too near) were a severe strain on resources throughout the week, but as Éamon Duggan later pointed out, they couldn't let them go.

> We could not afford to take the risk of spies informing our friend the enemy that we were holding that line with a handful of men and boys, a very mixed collection of firearms, very little ammunition and not a solitary machine gun.

In fact, the first prisoners taken, the DMP men who had been on duty in the Four Courts and the Bridewell, were released early in the grounds of the Richmond Asylum.

Morkan asserts that none of them used any of the information they must have gathered while being held.

The First Battalion ended the week with more prisoners than any other garrison. One of the officers held in the Four Courts recalled how they subsisted for several days on sherry, champagne, port, claret and Benedictine; although food was very scarce, the cellars were well stocked. Captain Brereton, quoted earlier, spoke highly of Daly's men in a later memoir, describing them as 'not out for massacre, burning or loot. They were out for war, observing all the rules of war and fighting men ....' He added, 'They treated their prisoners with the utmost courtesy and consideration, in fact, they proved by their conduct that they were men of courtesy and consideration, incapable of acts of brutality.'[16]

One of the more distinguished prisoners was Lord Dunsany, who was captured on Tuesday as he tried to make contact with Dublin Castle. Unaware of the extent of the Volunteer action, he was being driven along the quays with Lieutenant AP Lindsay when they were fired on at one of the barricades. His chauffeur was wounded, and he and Lindsay were taken prisoner. Lindsay was taken to the Four Courts, and later gave evidence at Daly's court martial. Daly had struck up an acquaintance with him, and taken him into his confidence, perhaps feeling the need for experienced advice.

Dunsany had been hit slightly in the face by a ricochet, and one of the Volunteers apologised for this. Their captain remarked jokingly that there was no danger of their entering 'The Glittering Gates' just yet, referring to a play by Dunsany, and Dunsany was delighted to find that he had been captured by literary men. Sent to Jervis Street hospital, he lay there for the rest of the week. Listening to the sounds of battle, he could tell when the tide began to turn – men were heard screaming, calling on God, and patient after patient was carried in, only to die.[17] Paddy Holahan later complimented him:

> I understand he [Dunsany] did a good turn later by ... lending his razor to several of our men, so that they might show the cheek of innocence to the British military when they started searching the hospital.[18]

On Friday night, all the prisoners in the Four Courts were taken to the Father Mathew Hall to be released, as well as the prisoners which had come from the Linen Hall Barracks. Daly requested them to forget all that they had seen. Prendergast remembered:

> Commandant Ned Daly ... as he always was – the perfect officer and soldier. Carrying a service rifle slung on his shoulder, he conducted the police to safety.

Johnny O'Connor (although he puts this event on the Saturday) said:

> I saw Ned Daly coming and he was with a body of men,

most of them in the uniform of the DMP, some of them in civilian clothes and some British army officers – about I think forty in all – and he was marching at their head ... It's quite clear, Ned Daly's object in bringing those men through our lines was that he didn't trust us as far as the DMP were concerned. He thought that we might have a crack at them on the way out and he personally conducted them the whole way.[19]

The Army Pay Corps prisoners from the Linen Hall Barracks had been taken to the Bridewell under heavy fire, and kept in three large cells. Later, a water main burst and threatened to drown them, but the leak was hastily repaired. A telephone call was received in the Bridewell during the week from Dublin Castle, which had not realised it was in rebel hands; the call was to warn the garrison to take cover in the cellars, as the Four Courts buildings were to be shelled.

Firing went on all night, and the barricade across North King Street at Coleraine Street was finally evacuated at about 3am.

The sound of crashing timber, the shouted commands of the officers in charge of the attack, the scream of bullets resounded continuously. Stabs of flame came from rifles and machine guns, the woodwork of windows was splintered, the bags of meal at loopholes were cut to pieces and spilled into the street.[20]

Éamon Duggan, battalion adjutant, recalled:

> Late on Friday night while the machine-gun rat-tat-tat
> was going on up the street, I was in the yard of the Four
> Courts. It was dark ... I saw a figure approaching me ...
> There was no one else in sight. We approached each other.
> It was Commandant Daly, come from HQ. I got a peculiar
> feeling that it was the beginning of the end.[21]

The atmosphere in the Four Courts was one of intense
strain, and symptoms of shock and fatigue were widely
observed among the men. One Volunteer went mad, and had
to be handcuffed to a bed. They were almost deaf from the
constant firing.

The Volunteers were aware that fierce fighting was taking
place in the North King Street area, but they had little idea
of the actual events of those dreadful days.

On Friday evening the British had begun artillery shelling of the Four Courts from the direction of Exchange
Street. They also took over Bolton Street technical schools,
and began to bring armoured cars into use. They had taken
motor lorries from Guinness's Brewery, and covered the
engines with iron plates. Old boilers on top contained soldiers. Each car would rush up a street, stop, and the soldiers would emerge from the boiler and storm the houses,
firing into them as they went. All through the King Street/
Church Street area this continued, through the night, and

the Volunteers contested each step, each room, each house. But by Saturday morning a number of King Street houses were occupied by the British. Local residents were rounded up and interrogated.

This was not all; it became clear when the Rising had ended and the smoke had cleared that dreadful events had happened in North King Street between Friday and Saturday. General Maxwell later said:

> Possibly unfortunate incidents, which we should regret now, may have occurred. It did not, perhaps, always follow that where shots were fired from a particular house the inmates were always necessarily aware of it, or guilty, but how were the soldiers to discriminate? They saw their comrades killed beside them by hidden and treacherous assailants, and it is even possible that under the horrors of this peculiar attack some of them 'saw red'.[22]

Three civilian men were shot in No. 170, two in No. 172 and two in No. 174. Four were shot in No. 24. Nothing was known of all this until 10 May, when two bodies were found hastily buried in the cellar of No. 177. In all, at least fifteen civilians had died. A military investigation was later carried out, and the witness statements make grim reading.

A city coroner's inquest ruled that two of the bodies found in shallow graves had been killed by soldiers, and were 'unarmed and unoffending' residents. It was conducted by Dr Louis A

Byrne, City Coroner, in the City Morgue, on Tuesday 16 May, and the bodies were those of Patrick Bealen (30) and James Healy (44). They had bullet wounds, and had been found in the cellar of No. 177 North King Street. Both were fully dressed, and were buried no more than twelve inches from the surface, obviously in haste. According to witnesses, Bealen, the foreman of the pub at No. 177, had been taken away in custody at midnight on 28 April. James Healy had been employed as a distiller by Jameson's, which during that week was a hotbed of Volunteer snipers. Bealen had evidently been shot from a distance, and Roseanna Knowles, who lived nearby and was later talking to one of the soldiers, is quoted as follows:

> [The soldier] said, 'I pitied him from my heart, though I had to shoot him. He had made tea for me.'... He said that when they brought him downstairs he had not the heart to shoot him straight, and that they told him (the deceased) to go upstairs again, and at the foot of the stairs they shot him – that they 'let bang' at the foot of the stairs.

It emerged at the later military inquiry that Bealen had been given a revolver by his employer, Mrs O'Reilly, to protect the house during the rebellion, and he had been seen boasting about shooting soldiers. Roseanna Knowles, questioned by the military about not having mentioned this at the inquest, said, 'Mrs O'Reilly told me before the inquest not to say anything except what I was asked.' Healy was said to have been suffering from delirium tremens during the week, 'running about the street'.[23] The military insisted that the fact of the bodies being buried in No. 177 was well known to all, and that the troops had been given instructions to bury all bodies they came across to prevent infection, but the witnesses insisted that the bodies were only found when the smell in the cellar became intolerable.

A statement by the O/C of the $2^{nd}/6^{th}$ South Staffordshire regiment, Lieutenant Colonel H Taylor, was read out at the coroner's inquest, and repudiated utterly any suggestion of unlawful killing, dwelling on the difficulties the soldiers faced in trying to gain control of North King Street. It had taken them from 10 o'clock on the morning on 28 April till 2pm on the 29th, and their casualties numbered eleven NCOs and men killed and over thirty wounded. He concluded:

> I am satisfied that during these operations the troops under my command showed great moderation and restraint under exceptionally difficult and trying circumstances.

The coroner was not so satisfied, and found:

> Patrick Bealen died from shock and haemorrhage, resulting from bullet wounds inflicted by a soldier, or soldiers, in whose custody he was, an unarmed and unoffending prisoner. We consider that the explanation given by the military authorities is very unsatisfactory, and we believe that if the

military authorities had any inclination they could produce the officer in charge.

The same finding was made in respect of James Healy.[24]

An identification parade of the whole battalion at Straffan camp gave witnesses an opportunity to identify the soldiers who had committed these crimes, but none could be identified with certainty. Indeed, the two men who shot Bealen and Healy had already been sent back to England, in haste, one of them a sergeant who, General Maxwell acknowledged in a letter to Lord Kitchener, 'acted like a madman, the redeeming feature being that he reported what he had done'.[25]

Many more tragic stories were told at the military court of enquiry, held in the last week of May. Mary Connolly, with a small hardware shop at 164 North King Street, recalled seeing her husband's body in No. 170, an unoccupied house, beside that of Mr Hickey, the local butcher, and the latter's son, aged sixteen:

> My husband was all shot about. Mr Hickey was also shot through the head and in his back.

Teresa Hickey had been searching frantically for her husband and son, and had found her son with one stab or bullet hole in the left side:

> When I had arranged the body, a soldier came up and said

I would have to go ... My husband was not a volunteer or in any way connected with them. He was a great Britisher ... [his] head was very much smashed about, and his clothes were ripped up the back and a bullet wound in the back of his hat.

On Saturday morning, Peadar Lawless and three older men were shot at the 'Louth Dairy', No. 27, after accusations that shots had been fired from the building. Mrs Lawless attested:

My son lay dead ... on the landing of the top-back room ... Poor Mr McCartney lay dead against the wall in a sitting position. Their brains had bespattered the curtains. Poor Finnegan was in the same relative sitting position, but had fallen dead across the bed. Patrick Hoey ... must have received fearful treatment as his head was burst open and lacerated.

A soldier apparently later said of McCartney:

The little man made a great struggle for his life and tried to throw himself out of a window, but we got him.[26]

At least fifteen civilians died in the course of the fighting in this small area; others included Michael Noonan (34), George Ennis (51), Michael Hughes and John Walsh (56). Mrs Walsh deposed:

I myself saw soldiers playing cards on a rug thrown over

my husband's dead body ... They were eating bully beef, drinking, laughing and jeering at everyone coming in ... My husband had been ten years in the army and was through the Boer War.

Mrs Beirnes, of 80 Church Street, speaking of the death of her husband John, recalled Edward Daly coming to and fro from the house during the week: 'on one occasion I made a cake for him and his men.' However, the street had become more dangerous, and the family had moved to the shelter of the North Dublin Union building, with many other refugees, leaving John behind. He was shot by a sniper as he made his way to Monks's bakery, where he looked after the horses.[27]

The military court of enquiry concluded that blame could not be ascribed to ordinary soldiers, because of a lack of witnesses. This was widely seen as a whitewash. A confidential assessment later implied that, because the soldiers had been ordered not to take prisoners, they had interpreted this as an order to shoot suspected rebels. However, Irish public opinion saw these as murders, committed not in the heat of battle but in a cold-blooded follow-up operation, in charge of officers. Many of the soldiers involved had also taken part in the fighting at Mount Street Bridge, earlier in the week, when a group of Sherwood Foresters was almost wiped out by Third Battalion snipers in the surrounding houses, and they would have been further enraged by that memory.[28]

Writing to Field Marshal Earl Kitchener, Secretary for

War, Maxwell implied that the civilian witnesses had been influenced by solicitors and others to put the worst case possible, and were probably untruthful. Kitchener seemed to have difficulty in believing British soldiers could have behaved so badly:

> Do you not consider it to be much more likely that Sinn Féiners who were holding the houses were shot by our men from outside and, before our men entered, were buried by their comrades, or that altercations regarding surrender may have occurred amongst the Sinn Féiners resulting in those who disagreed with the majority being shot and buried. If our men shot others in hot blood I cannot think that they would bury them also.[29]

Indeed, this 'hot blood'/'seeing red' argument would imply strongly that ungoverned violence *had* taken place, and that the burials were, as suspected by public opinion, hasty attempts to hide the evidence under official authority when matters had gone too far to be ignored.

Announcing the results of the enquiry to the House of Commons, the prime minister admitted:

> There can be little doubt that some men who were not taking an actual part in the fighting were in the course of the struggle killed by both rebels and soldiers. But after careful inquiry it is impossible to bring home responsibility to any particular person or persons.[30]

At dawn on Saturday morning, a British attack was made on the barricade facing Bolton Street, but met with a hot reception. The attackers, twelve to fifteen British soldiers, rushed into Beresford Street to escape, but found themselves faced by another barricade, and covered both by the men in the partly-built cottages backing onto Beresford Street, and by the snipers in the Malt House tower. The British party was almost wiped out, and their rifles and about a hundred rounds of ammunition were retrieved. Many of the rifles, however, had been shattered by the Volunteers' fire, and were useless. This was the last open attack by the military, who proceeded thereafter by tunnelling or mouse-holing from house to house. The barricade at Beresford Street was evacuated early in the day, but the Malt House snipers held out till 3pm. A line of retreat over the roofs brought the survivors to the Four Courts.[31]

Also on Saturday morning, about 5am, Michael O'Flanagan's section of C Company in Reilly's Fort faced the end of their ammunition supplies. Volunteers made a desperate dash to the Father Mathew Hall, under intense machine-gun fire, and managed to get some ammunition and grenades, but this cost the life of Michael's brother Patrick. Meanwhile, they were being completely cut off by the North Staffs. As the morning wore on, Lieutenant Collins unwillingly decided that the time had come to evacuate, and he ordered a desperate charge across to the barricade outside the Father Mathew Hall. As they abandoned Reilly's Fort, it was taken over by the British troops in North King Street.

Fourteen men made it safely, with a couple of injuries. They were given covering fire by men of F Company under Frank Shouldice, and joined these men at the barricade to continue firing. Michael O'Flanagan was then approached by Commandant Ned Daly, and instructed to withdraw his men and proceed to the Four Courts to reinforce the garrison there. On the way O'Flanagan found his company captain, Frank Fahy, lying near the Four Courts entrance; he had suffered a heart attack. They managed to get him into the building, where he was looked after by Cumann na mBan members.

Volunteers attempted to encircle the soldiers now holding Reilly's Fort, and Ball's drug store was occupied in order to outflank them. Fighting became concentrated into fifty yards of Upper Church Street, between North King Street and North Brunswick Street. As soldiers appeared into Church Street, they came under fire from Clarke's dairy, Moore's coach factory, and the barricades near the church. Some took cover in Blanchardstown Bakery, but came under continual fire. A young soldier fell into the street, and the Volunteers offered to cease firing so he could be removed, but the sergeant-major in charge refused, with much bad language. Shortly afterwards the sergeant-major was also shot, and a brief cease-fire enabled both bodies to be recovered.[32]

The Volunteers in Clarke's Dairy realised that Reilly's Fort had been taken by the British, and that they were completely cut off. They continued to fight, causing severe casualties to the South Staffs. Laffan, in Moore's Factory, trying to guide some of his men to safety from a reconnaissance, was wounded in the head as he leaned out of a window, and had to retire to the Richmond Hospital. Lieutenant P Breslin took his place.[33] Volunteer snipers were kept busy, as they were pinned down under heavy fire. Patrick Kelly of G Company recalled:

> I had a bale of curled hair propped against the window for cover. One of my comrades shouted to me about something. I turned round to ask what he wanted. The action saved my life, for when I turned back ... I found that a bullet had passed through on a level with my chest, leaving a string of curled hair protruding from the bale.

Lieutenant Breslin wanted to reinforce the Volunteers on the opposite side of the street, and Kelly and two others tried to get across. Kelly made it alone, managing to scale a backyard ladder to an upper floor. He helped the four men in the house to break through into neighbouring houses with an axe, and they continued their sniping activities through the windows until word came of the surrender, about 7.30pm.

Late that Saturday morning, in the Four Courts, the officers held a conference, and decided to make a counter-attack that night, apparently aimed at Wellington Barracks.[34] 'The officers to accompany Commandant Daly were detailed', said Éamon Duggan. 'It was my honour to be one of them. Everyone wanted to be where he went. He was idolised by officers and men alike.' Daly was then called away by Joseph McDonough of C Company.

All that week, according to McDonough, Fr O'Callaghan of Arran Quay had been going among C Company trying to persuade the men to lay down their arms:

> Lt Thomas Allen … asked him for God's sake to go away and leave us alone. Despite this request, he persisted in his activity, but nevertheless he heard our confessions when asked to do so.

On Saturday about 1pm, Fr O'Callaghan and a British officer came towards them, and McDonough arrested the officer and sent for Commandant Daly. Daly was informed by the officer that Pearse had surrendered, and was given a typed document with Pearse's signature. Nurse Elizabeth O'Farrell, who had conveyed Pearse's surrender to General Lowe earlier that day, states that she herself, accompanied by Fr Columbus of Church Street, brought the surrender order to Edward Daly: 'He was very much cut up about it but accepted his orders as a soldier should.'[35]

Saying, 'Very well, it is the fortune of war,' Daly saluted the British officer and handed over his sword; he did not consult with his officers. He beckoned Piaras Béaslaí into the private room of the battalion staff, and handed him Pearse's letter: 'His head was buried in his hands. He was weeping.'

Annie Fahy heard her husband telling his men to cease fire, but hold on to their guns. 'Later I saw Ned without his sword. He just shook his head.' That was the last she saw of her husband until the autumn, when Madge and Agnes Daly took her to Portland Prison to visit him.

A Canadian journalist who got caught up in the fighting in Dublin that week, and later wrote an account of the Rising, said of the Four Courts garrison:

> They were finally completely penned up, for any attempt to move in the open brought heavy fire from the surrounding troops. Here, again, the influence of the Catholic clergy was called in with great effect, and Daly, learning what had happened at the GPO, made his surrender, with a generous request that the punishment for what had taken place might fall on himself and not on his followers.[36]

At some point during the afternoon, Ned Daly made his way back to the convent in North Brunswick Street, according to a statement by Sister Agnes of that convent, written in 1966. He asked her to look after his gun, as a favour, and she hid it under a couch in the hall. However, her superior found it and insisted that she hand it over to the Master of the North Dublin Union, where she was working. The Master was very excited to receive the gun, and hid it in a drawer. Two days later, Sister Agnes asked to use his phone; removing the gun from the drawer, she hid it up her sleeve. She gave it to a priest from Howth, County Dublin, who buried it in a garden. Some years later it was given back to Sister Agnes, who presented it to the Daly family. This gun is now in the National Museum of Ireland.[37]

As word spread of the surrender, the surviving members of the First Battalion began to come in, in ones and twos, from the various outposts. Seán Prendergast, captain of C Company, said in his witness statement:

> All looked as if they had gone 'through the mill' during the past few days, some worse than others. It was in their faces, their general appearance, and even their clothes showed signs that they had been campaigning. Some were unwashed, unkempt, dust from head to feet.

Daly went to the main hall, where the men were gathering. Some of them were very angry, demanding to fight to the death and vowing never to surrender their weapons. Daly said:

> I have my orders from my Commander-in-Chief. I have given my sword and my word to the British officer and nobody shall go back on it.

Father Augustine warned them that if they did not surrender they would be wiped out, but Daly replied:

> We don't give a damn about that, Father. We must sur-
> render because we have the order from our Commander-
> in-Chief.[38]

Brigid Lyons Thornton reported the 'terrible confusion'
at that time:

> I said I'd go [home], but then Ned Daly came in and said,
> 'Listen, don't go, the city's under martial law.' That was the
> first time I'd ever actually spoken to him ... 'Lieutenant
> Lindsay here' – that was one of the British officers – 'has
> given me his word of honour that all you girls will be taken
> home in the morning.' Lieutenant Lindsay was quite an
> attractive young man, nicely dressed in uniform ... and I
> said, 'Whatever you say, Commandant, I'll do.'

The girls remained upstairs for the night, listening to criti-
cism from some of the Church Street priests, and were taken
to Richmond Barracks the following day. That evening they
were marched to Kilmainham Gaol, through abusive crowds
of 'separation women', and put three or four to a cell. Lieutenant Lindsay had failed to come through.[39]

Members of Cumann na mBan in the Father Mathew
Hall took the opportunity of the lull in fighting to remove
the wounded to the Richmond Hospital, carrying them on
stretchers. Those more lightly wounded managed to escape.
Four of the women spent the rest of that night in the church
next to the Hall, and managed to escape after attending Mass

on the Sunday morning and mingling with the crowd. They noticed several Volunteers among the congregation, who obviously had the same plan in mind.

Michael T Foy and Brian Barton, in their account of the Rising, say:

> It was saving the lives of civilians and especially women and children that Daly stressed and, while he admitted with surprising candour having been beaten by a superior force, he reassured the garrison that they had done their duty and could carry themselves with pride after redeeming Ireland's name.[40]

Brigid Thornton witnessed men in the courtyard who tried to destroy their guns rather than surrender them: 'I could see them hacking away at them.'[41] Many of them were weeping. The arms and ammunition were handed through the railings to the soldiers waiting outside.

Éamon Morkan's witness statement recalled:

> I realise now that I was most unreasonable, and at first refused to hand up arms and ammunition. I think this feeling can be explained by ... the belief that we must not under any circumstances surrender the arms and equipment which we had made so much effort to obtain.[42]

Johnny O'Connor, arriving in the Four Courts after receiving the message of surrender, observed:

[Daly] could have escaped in the end or disguised himself, because he hadn't been a signatory of the proclamation and he would have stood a very good chance of getting through altogether. He didn't bother about that. He came and surrendered his men and he dressed in the full uniform of a commandant. As you can imagine he looked very well in the uniform. He knew how to wear it – you'd think he was born in a uniform.

... He came down along the lines and he picked out several men ... that were not dressed in uniform and he told them to clear out and get through this hole in the wall we had, and get away and ... at least twelve did get away ... I'm mentioning that just to show that he was always thinking of the men under him – never thought of himself. As I said before – a perfect gentleman. Every man in the First Battalion, I think, would willingly have given his life for Ned Daly. There was never a finer man to lead any parties than he was.[43]

Joseph McDonough said that Lieutenant Joe McGuinness also advised them to make a run for it, if possible, and McDonough managed to make his way to safety and discard his uniform.

O'Connor continued:

It seemed to me then perfectly clear ... that Ned Daly's object, in getting us into the Four Courts, was he didn't want to have us surrendering in isolated groups. He was afraid that we might get badly handled by the British. He wanted to do the thing in the proper form and manner. Dressed in his full uniform he paraded us in the Four Courts and then sent word to the British to come in. The British soldiers filed in and they surrounded us.[44]

Another Volunteer says that Daly's last words to them were, 'This is not the end of the fight for Irish freedom – it is the beginning.'[45]

The officer in charge asked Daly to order his men to march, and he did, saying with a sad smile, according to Duggan, 'Now boys, for the last time.' They trooped off, singing the rebel songs they normally sang on marches. The Volunteers from other areas who had already surrendered had been brought to O'Connell Street, where they were lined up.

Éamonn Dore wrote: 'one outstanding memory remains of that Easter Saturday evening':

It was the sound of marching men. Into the street from Abbey Street came the old First Battalion with their loved Commandant, Ned Daly, leading. Still the same quiet, calm, self-possessed Ned, unconquered and unconquerable as his men, marching four deep behind him. He brought them up O'Connell Street, dropped out when he came to his allotted position and then drilled his men, leaving them two deep 'standing easy'... I heard a British sergeant say to another,

'That's an officer and those fellows know their stuff.

A British officer roared, 'Who is in charge of this party?'
Two heels clicked. Ned Daly took two paces forward and
said in a loud voice, 'I am.'[46]

Piaras Béaslaí reported that Daly replied, 'I am. At all
events, I was,' which he must have known would be his death
warrant. Seán Kennedy recalled a British officer taking the
names of the prisoners, and quietly warning them that if
they had anything incriminating on them, they should drop
it at their feet. They were then marched on to the Rotunda
Gardens.

Seán McLoughlin, who had been part of the escape from the
GPO and the surrender in Moore Street, watched the relays of
surrendered Volunteers arriving in the Rotunda Gardens.

An officer which proved to be Ned Daly was thrown on
the ground beside us ... He said, '...What on earth happened, Seán. Why have we surrendered?' I said, "Don't ask
me. Ask Sean McDermott here, he will tell you,' but Sean
would not speak. We carried on a desultory conversation in
low tones. Every time this officer saw us make a move or
speak, he swore and cursed and threatened us.

McLoughlin told Daly all he could about the events of the
week. Daly said, 'I don't think we were beaten. I think we
had still plenty of fight left in us yet.'[47]

Jim O'Sullivan, Ned's close friend, was also in the Rotunda, having surrendered in Moore Street, but they do not seem to have spoken. Jim ends his official witness statement with his arrival at the Rotunda, and goes no further. It may well have been too painful. He would talk to his children and grandchildren in later years about his experiences in prison, but only mentioned Ned in reminiscences of their years of friendship, saying nothing about Ned's part in the Rising, its aftermath, or the executions.

About four hundred surrendered fighters spent a miserable night in the Rotunda Gardens, and there are several accounts of bad treatment suffered by some of them. Tom Sheerin is among many who observed Tom Clarke being ill-treated by one officer, Captain Percival Lea-Wilson. Clarke is reported to have been stripped naked to be searched, in front of the windows of the nurses' home in the Rotunda. Lea-Wilson was later shot during the War of Independence, apparently on the order of Michael Collins, who had been a witness of this treatment.[48]

Seán Kennedy says that Lea-Wilson also mistreated Edward Daly: 'I remember seeing him ripping the epaulettes from Daly's tunic in a most insulting and threatening manner.' Morkan recounts that Daly was searched the next morning, and his papers and personal belongings thrown on the ground.

An NCO passing by was requested by Daly to allow him to pick up the papers. The NCO handed the items back

163

and when the officer in charge [Lea-Wilson] later found that the ground had been cleared he shouted loudly for the NCO responsible, soundly rated him and asked him was he 'a bloody servant to the rebels'.

Another account says that a British soldier was shouted at by a Captain Cherry for lending Daly a handkerchief.[49] Louis Le Roux suggests that Ned Daly was stripped as Clarke was, and put through 'a cruel form of search'. This is also asserted by Éamonn Dore.[50]

The prisoners were kept seated on the damp ground, cramped together in the small green space, for the whole night. There was no food, nor were they allowed sanitary facilities; there were some Cumann na mBan present, but the sexes were not separated. The next morning, about 9am, they were marched to Richmond Barracks, near Kilmainham Gaol. They were astounded at the damage they witnessed as they walked through the city centre; they had not fully realised the extent of the devastation caused.

At the barracks they stood in the yard for about two hours in hot weather, and many of them collapsed from exhaustion and hunger. They were searched, and watches, rosary beads, cash and other items of value were removed, few of which were returned. Many of the soldiers who guarded them were Irish – friends and relatives were recognised, and some soldiers expressed sympathy, stating that if the Rebellion had waited till the war was over, they would have joined in.

G-Men, the detectives of the DMP, had spent the morning picking out men of interest to them, and these remained in custody while the other Volunteers were deported. Along with the signatories of the Proclamation and the Volunteer commandants, the ninety eventually chosen included Frank Shouldice and Jim O'Sullivan. Taken to Kilmainham Gaol for court-martial, about a week after the surrender, they heard the firing-squads which killed their leaders, and expected that this would also be their fate. However, all of them had their sentences commuted to five years' penal servitude, and they eventually ended up in prisons and prison camps in Britain.

Some Volunteers had not surrendered that Saturday night. Patrick Kelly's unit stayed in Church Street/North Brunswick Street until Sunday morning. They were waiting for a written order from Pearse, and had agreed to a temporary cease-fire until it arrived. When the surrender was confirmed in the morning, Paddy Holahan addressed the men briefly, and then was asked by the British colonel in charge to turn out the rest of them. Much to the colonel's chagrin, Holahan made it clear that the fifty-eight men and boys he could see were all that there were; they had held off a whole British battalion for three days. They dumped their arms in North King Street: 'After parting with my rifle I felt sad as if I had lost a very dear comrade.' They were brought into Richmond Barracks, and eventually into the gymnasium there, where they found the rest of the surrendered fighters.

Edward Daly could be proud of the battle he had fought, and the men he had led. An assessment by Major-General PJ Hally of the Irish army later said of his command:

> In my opinion, Daly showed excellent military skill by concentrating his force when he knew his small mobilisation strength; by organising local attacks to retake ground lost; by establishing strong points such as Reilly's pub at the corner of North King Street and Church Street, mutually supported by fire from other posts such as Jameson's Malt House. To sum up, this was an excellent area – well held and well defended.[51]

Chapter Six

• • • • • •

1916 Legacy

Achievement?

he great adventure had come to an end, and on the morning of Sunday, 30 April, a long line of bedraggled men and women marched, proudly and defiantly, towards the prison gates, ignoring the contemptuous jeers of Dublin's citizens. They spent the night in the gymnasium of Richmond Barracks, Inchicore.

Volunteer Paddy Kelly recalled seeing Edward Daly:

Seated along the floor by the wall I noticed Comdt. MacDonagh and Comdt. E. Daly. They looked tired and sad. As I looked at Comdt. Daly he gave me a sad smile and that was the last I ever saw of him.[1]

The G-men and DMP constables continued the task of identifying the ringleaders, as well as other persons of interest. The G-men were obviously enjoying their work, but

167

many of the DMP refused to identify rebels. Some of the prisoners who had been held by the rebels also refused to identify their captors.

Brian O'Higgins recognised Ned Daly in the gymnasium, and described him as:

> ... grimy as the rest of us, a turban made of a silk scarf about his head, his uniform very much the worse for wear. He smiled his old smile when our eyes met, shook his head, sadly, as if to say: 'Pity it wasn't a fight to the finish,' and then pulled himself together like a man that had been dreaming. He was every inch a soldier as he had always been, and there was no sign of defeat or dread about him. No wonder his men almost worshipped him and were ready to face anything under his intrepid leadership.[2]

Liam Ó Briain, also held in Richmond Barracks, said in his memoirs that Ned Daly sang that night to keep up everyone's spirits, a cheerful and spirited version of a Gilbert and Sullivan song.[3]

Over 3,400 people were arrested as a result of the Rising, of whom 1,400 or so were released over the next two weeks. Approximately 1,600 were marched down to the docks over the following twenty-four hours, and embarked for prisons and prison camps in Britain. Many of the Cumann na mBan women had to insist on their right to be arrested, and they were taken to Richmond Barracks and Ship Street

Barracks. Ultimately only seven women were deported to Britain, including Dr Kathleen Lynn and Countess Markievicz. The others, about seventy of them, were released, under the assumption that they had not had political convictions; General Maxwell declared that he was happy to be rid of 'all those silly little girls', and he was sure the right thing to do was to send them home.[4]

General Sir John Maxwell was a retired officer who had been recalled to duty when the First World War broke out. Sent to Ireland as 'Military Governor' to deal with the Easter Rising, he arrived on 28 April. The leaders of the Dublin Castle administration, Lord Wimborne, Augustine Birrell and Sir Matthew Nathan, strongly resented their loss of power to the military, and all sent in their resignations as soon as the fighting ended. Maxwell thus found himself unwillingly in supreme command.

There were many voices urging caution in dealing with the prisoners. The Prime Minister, HH Asquith, received a telegram from the about-to-resign Castle administration, requesting that martial law not be established, because of the risk of inflaming public opinion. The government, however, wanted to look authoritative and in control, and confirmed Maxwell's extension of martial law, but Maxwell himself knew that many politicians were unhappy with the decision. In Dublin and aware of the tense atmosphere John Dillon, an MP of the Irish Parliamentary Party, wrote to its leader, John Redmond:

> You should urge strongly on the government the *extreme* unwisdom of any wholesale shooting of prisoners ... If there were shootings of prisoners on any large scale the effect on public opinion might be disastrous in the extreme.[5]

German contacts with the Rising complicated matters. Treason was even more treasonous in time of war, and the leaders would have to be made an example of. Under the Defence of the Realm Acts, Maxwell did have the authority to court-martial civilians. However, he also held the court martials in secret, which was later held to have been illegal. At each court martial, evidence was heard by three officer judges, who might or might not have had legal training. A death sentence had to be unanimous, and confirmed by Maxwell himself. Accurate written records were kept; some defendants' questions to prosecution witnesses were not recorded, but the responses were. Most of the trials lasted for no more than ten or fifteen minutes, and the accused were not allowed any legal representation.[6]

Maxwell ultimately classified the cases for court martial under three headings:

> (a) Those who signed proclamation on behalf of provisional Government and were also leaders in actual rebellion in Dublin.

(b) Those who were in command of rebels actually shooting down troops, police and others.

(c) Those whose offence was murder.

Edward Daly was placed in category (b), along with two
other battalion commanders, Michael Mallin and Seán
Heuston. Ned Daly's court martial was held in Richmond
Barracks. The majority of the court martials were held there;
James Connolly was tried in Dublin Castle and Thomas Kent
in Cork Detention Barracks.

The list of those executed contains many inconsistencies,
and the rationale behind it is puzzling. Michael O'Hanrahan
seems to have been condemned because he had been 'arrested
in uniform and armed', which would describe almost everyone held in Richmond Barracks.[7] Not every commandant
was executed – Éamon de Valera was spared, but that may
have been because he was tried late in the sequence, when
an outcry was already arising against the executions. There
might have been a chance for Edward Daly, as he had not
signed the Proclamation. However, his close relationship
with Thomas Clarke probably helped to sway the verdict.
Besides, he had run a very effective command.

Before his own execution, in the early morning of 3 May,
Tom Clarke asked if he could see Ned Daly before he died.
However, as Daly was considered a very important prisoner,
there was a lot of delay in getting permission to bring him

from Richmond Barracks in time. Tom was on his way to execution just as Ned arrived, but Ned insisted that he would see him dead or alive. Clarke, Patrick Pearse and Thomas Mac-Donagh were executed one after another, and their bodies placed in the shed used by prisoners to break stones.

> Daly went out to this shed, stood to attention and saluted the remains. He then took off his cap, knelt down and prayed for some time. He put on his cap again, saluted again and returned to his escort.[8]

That same day, 3 May, Edward Daly was led to his own court martial in Richmond Barracks. The charge was the same for all of them:

> Did an act to wit did take part in an armed rebellion and in the waging of war against His Majesty the King such act being of such a nature as to be calculated to be prejudicial to the Defence of the Realm and being done with the intention and for the purpose of assisting the enemy.

When charged, Daly pleaded 'Not guilty', as did all the condemned men, except for Patrick Pearse.

The first witness for the prosecution was Lieutenant Halpin, of the Third Sherwood Foresters, who had been one of the prisoners detained in the Four Courts.

> I first saw the accused on Thursday April 27 – he was armed and in uniform. I don't know if he was in authority.

Cross-examined by the accused, he stated:

> I first saw the accused in the room in which I was detained
> and he asked if I was properly treated. And on the second
> occasion he told me there was a danger of the wing in
> which I was being shelled and he had me removed. On the
> third occasion he asked me if I had my meals and bedding
> all right.

The second witness was Lieutenant AP Lindsay, of the
Fifth Battalion, Inniskillen Fusiliers. He had been arrested
on Tuesday 25 April, and said he had been fired on prior to
arrest. He stated:

> I saw the accused during my confinement. I did not see
> the accused give any orders. I saw him on Thursday, Friday
> and Saturday, and had conversation with him. On Saturday
> I was informed that Commandant Daly wanted to see me
> and I went down to see him ... He said he intended to make
> a counter-attack as the position was hopeless. I told him it
> was useless and that he had better surrender. He said that he
> could not surrender without orders from his superior.

In a later memoir, Lord Dunsany said of Lieutenant Lindsay:

> [His] rather overbearing manner and lack of respect for
> authority particularly showed themselves when, a prisoner
> in the Four Courts, captured by the Sinn Féiners, he asked
> to be shewn the plans of the Sinn Féin army. These were

shewn to him, and brushing them aside with the same excess of confidence in which I had seen him indulge in the presence of his own senior officers, he said, 'Those plans are no good. You'd better surrender.' And they did.[9]

Dunsany was of course overstating the case; Daly would never have surrendered without an order from his direct superior.

Cross-examined by Daly, Lindsay said:

He told me he had had a conference with the officers and that a counter-attack had been decided upon. He also said that he did not expect anyone who took part in this counter-attack would come back alive. He said the object of making this counter-attack was to save the lives of as many people as possible in the building.

Daly resisted absolutely any suggestion of aiding the enemy in a time of war.

In his defence, Edward Daly said:

The reason I pleaded 'Not guilty' was because I had no dealings with any outside forces. I had no knowledge of the insurrection until Monday morning April 24. The officers including myself when we heard the news held a meeting and decided that the whole thing was foolish but that being under orders we had no option but to obey.

In a report on the executions sent to Lord Kitchener on

11 May, General Maxwell said of Edward Daly:

> This man was one of the most prominent extremists in the
> Sinn Féin organisation. He held the rank of Commandant
> and was in command of the body of rebels who held the
> Four Courts where heavy fighting took place and casualties
> occurred. He admitted being at the meeting of officers who
> decided to carry out the order of the executive council and
> commence the armed rebellion.[10]

It is probable that his close relationship with Tom Clarke
was also taken into consideration, but it would not have been
known that Daly was in the IRB.

Commandant Edward Daly was found guilty, and sentenced to 'death by being shot'. Each prisoner was removed
from Richmond Barracks to Kilmainham Gaol the night
before his execution.

Three of Ned Daly's sisters, Madge, Kathleen and Laura,
were brought to Kilmainham to see him that night. Kathleen had already visited to say goodbye to her husband Tom
Clarke, and knew that he had been shot that morning. The
sentry at Ned's cell was shocked to see her, recognising her
from the previous night. They found their brother asleep on
the hard floor, exhausted.

Laura, the youngest of them, the one to whom Ned was
closest, never wrote an account of that last meeting, but she
commented once to her daughter that his face and hands

were 'black', presumably from gunfire. She would have been very struck by seeing him dirty and dishevelled, since he was normally so dapper. Kathleen describes the meeting briefly in her memoir, but states that she stayed at the door of the cell talking to the soldiers, to prevent them from hearing anything private Ned might have to say, so she heard very little of the conversation.

Madge, the eldest, later wrote an article detailing these last moments with their brother. The dialogue comes across as stilted, possibly embroidered with the passage of time, but the account is accurate in its essential details. She described how they 'shook to pieces' and could not stop crying during the journey to the prison, but pulled themselves together as they walked in the door, hearing the jailer call, 'Relatives of Daly, to be shot in the morning.'

The first thing Ned said to them was, 'I did my best,' and he talked about his men and how well they had fought – such heroes never lived, he said, and they had only lost heart at the order to surrender. At his court martial, he continued, he had strongly protested the accusation of 'aiding the enemy'. His only regret was the surrender. He had realised it was an honourable one and had agreed to it, otherwise they would all have fought to the end. Kathleen heard him say, 'It doesn't matter – we had planned to go out on a job on Saturday night in which we all expected to go down.'[11]

When asked if he had food, he pointed to some biscuits

thrown on the floor. He spoke also of the prisoners the Volunteers had held, and how they had treated them with courtesy and consideration. Laura exclaimed, 'Why did you not do as they are now doing to you – shoot them?' 'Ah no, Laura,' he replied, 'that would not be playing the game fair. We all got strict orders that all prisoners were to be treated under the rules of civilised warfare as prisoners of war and as kindly as possible under the conditions.'

Most of the condemned men gave souvenirs to their grieving families during their last hours – they cut off their buttons and emptied their pockets. They had all been searched on their arrest, and some items of value were never recovered. Ned apparently gave Laura his buttons, but their whereabouts are unknown; she may have deposited them with a museum. The sisters asked Ned about his watch, but according to Madge he said, 'A gentleman kindly relieved me of it.'

Nora Daly (later Dore), recounting what her sisters told her after the event, said that Ned had actually given his watch to Lieutenant AP Lindsay as a reward. Lindsay had promised to take care of a sum of money in gold which John Daly had given to Ned for use during the Rising, and to return it to Ned's mother.[12] Lindsay apparently did not do this, and Madge eventually had to threaten to tell the story in public. The money was later returned, in currency notes rather than in gold.

In the end, it was a very small collection the sisters received. A group of items, consisting of a notecase, a toothbrush, a pencil and a tobacco pipe, was found unexpectedly in a desk drawer during the writing of this book, having been mislaid for many years. The note of explanation with them was written by Éamonn Dore, who married Nora Daly after the Rising, and says that these items 'were used by Ned Daly during the fighting Easter Week. Given to his sisters just before he was shot'. Éamonn later passed them on to his son Éamonn Óg, who died suddenly, prematurely young, not having told anyone where they were.[13] The silver-bound notecase contains part of a return railway ticket to Limerick, dated 24 December 1914, but nothing else. The items are all of good quality, and obviously expensive: the toothbrush handle is of ivory, and the pipe has a silver binding and an amber mouthpiece. Ned was living up to his reputation of always being well turned-out.

The sisters also mention a purse with some coins, and another pencil. These are no longer extant. There may well have been several items, such as rosary beads, brought home to Ned's mother. These would have been lost in the Black and Tan raid of 1921 which burned the contents of the family home. Although the sisters do not mention it, the National Museum of Ireland contains a first-aid kit, described as given by Ned to his sister Laura before his execution: 'Cloth bag, printed black on outside "First Field Dressing"... Contents –

gauze and wool pad.' It had been used by Cumann na mBan member Mary O'Sullivan in the Four Courts. The story of Ned's gun has already been told (Chapter 5), and it is now in the National Museum. Another gun of his was lent by Laura to Limerick Museum many years ago, and was later stolen.

A soldier called, 'Time's up' after fifteen minutes. Kathleen objected, saying she had had much longer with her husband the night before, but no extra time was allowed. Ned's sisters hugged him for the last time, as he sent messages to his mother and the rest of the family. Madge quoted him as saying, 'Tell Uncle John I did my best' before they left, but one of the few things Laura ever said about this last meeting, years later, was that Ned deliberately sent no message to John. Madge may have been trying to spare John's feelings by inventing this quote, but neither of her sisters ever contradicted it on record. It was a brief meeting, of heightened and intense emotion, and it would be no wonder if recollections differed.

As Kathleen kissed Ned goodbye, he asked whether she had received Tom's body; she thought it an odd request. She said she had not, but was going to request it, and that Madge would ask for his. In the event, none of the families received the bodies of the men executed at Kilmainham Gaol; they were buried in quicklime in a mass grave in Arbour Hill Barracks, in order to prevent a series of martyrs' funerals. Nora says that Laura asked to be allowed to send in a coffin, but this was refused. She also asked to get his uniform back, but was told that he would be buried in it.

The sisters were escorted from the cell, and driven back to Kathleen's home. They passed cars containing the relatives of the others due for execution that morning – Michael O'Hanrahan (whose sisters they met on the way out), Joseph Plunkett and William Pearse. Madge later wrote:

> The rest of that night is our own and God's; but we did not miss one moment of agony. We counted every second until dawn, when our heroes' souls flew to their reward.[14]

At 3am on the morning of 4 May, four Capuchin Friars were called on to give the condemned men the last rites. Father Columbus Murphy, one of the Capuchin fathers, described visiting Ned Daly. As he entered the cell, he saw a look of relief and gladness on the prisoner's face. Ned made his confession and received Holy Communion with great fervour, and prepared for death. Fr Columbus had to hurry to another part of the jail to give communion to Joseph Plunkett, and was just in time to do so. Returning to Daly's cell, he found he was too late to see him again; he heard the shots of the execution. He and the other friars were driven back to their church, where they celebrated Mass for the souls of the deceased.[15]

In the next cell was Dinny O'Callaghan, who later told his wife that Ned Daly knocked at his door on the way past, and said, 'Goodbye, Dinny'.[16] A Catholic priest wrote:

> I remember well seeing Commandant Daly coming down
> from the prison cell ... He was calm and brave as when
> he was with his men in the Church Street area, and asked
> to be remembered to the Sisters of Charity in Brunswick
> Street, who were known to him and had been very kind.
> As I shook his hand for the last time I felt intensely all that
> was meant by marching out blindfolded to his death such a
> gentle, noble, brave young Irishman.[17]

Seán MacDiarmada, due to die on 12 May, wrote a final
letter to his old friend John Daly, to say goodbye. He added:

> God guard and protect you all in No. 15. You have had a
> sore trial, but I know quite well that Mrs Daly and all the
> girls feel proud in spite of a little temporary and natural
> grief, that her son, and the girls' brother, as well as Tom, are
> included in the list of heroes.

Each prisoner had a piece of white paper pinned above
the heart, to guide the firing party. Each squad consisted of
twelve soldiers, and the executions were witnessed by the
prison governor and doctor.

> The first man to be shot will be brought out at 3.45 am
> facing the firing party of one officer, and 12 men at 10
> paces distant.

The rifles of the firing party will be loaded by other men behind their backs, 1 rifle with a blank cartridge, and eleven with ball, and the firing party will be told that this is the arrangement, and no man is to know which rifle is loaded with blank. There will be 4 firing parties, who will fire in turn.

After each prisoner has been shot, a Medical Officer will certify that he is dead, and his body will be immediately removed to an ambulance, with a label pinned on his breast giving his name ...[18]

Sentence was carried out with the customary military precision, a report being made by Major-General AE Sandbach, commanding the 59th Division:

I have to report that the following prisoners were executed between 4 am and 4.30 this morning:

Name	Case No.
Edward Daly	21
William Pearse	27
Joseph Plunkett	33
Michael O'Haurehan [r. O'Hanrahan]	36

... The sentence was promulgated in accordance with your orders in each case and the proceedings are endorsed accordingly.

Also enclosed are (1) certificate of execution by the
Acting APM of this Division, (2) Sketch of the position
of the graves, and (3) certificate of death by the medical
officer.[19]

Ned's mother, Catharine Daly, when told of his execution,
thanked God for giving her the honour of being the mother
of such a noble Irishman. Over a year later, she wrote from 15
Barrington Street, Limerick on 20 September 1917, asking
for a report of the court-martial proceedings. This request
was refused on 24 September 1917, because the court martial
was held in camera, 'and it has been decided on grounds of
public interest that the proceedings can not be published.'[20]

John Daly died in Limerick on 30 June 1916, aged seventy.
Already in poor health, he had been shattered by the executions of his nephew Ned and his close friends Tom Clarke
and Seán MacDiarmada. He left an estate valued at £2,390
(at a time when the average weekly wage was £1).

The worth of the Easter Rising will be debated as long as
Irish history is remembered – was it all just a waste? Could
independence have been achieved more peacefully, with a
little more patience? There is little doubt that it was not the
Rising itself which transformed Irish public opinion, but the
British military response, which was seen as disproportion-
ate and heavy-handed. The executions, in particular, brought
forth a wave of sympathy for the condemned men and for
their families, and the internment camps in Britain acted as

training grounds for the next round of hostilities, the War of Independence.

Speaking of Michael Mallin, Brian Hughes has said, 'it is, unsurprisingly, almost impossible to find negative comments from veterans about any executed leader.'[21] Even given this, many of the remarks in the Bureau of Military History witness statements about Edward Daly could almost be termed 'gushing'. They dwell on his good looks and military bearing, his cool and calm demeanour, his courage under fire, his ability to inspire his men to the highest endeavour – they would die in his defence if necessary. He is portrayed as embodying all the best qualities of a hero.

These statements were, of course, made by men and women, thirty years after the Rising, who had lived through the subsequent War of Independence, the bitter and divisive Civil War, and the struggles and compromises inseparable from the development of a new, independent nation. Ned Daly epitomised the ideals they had fought for in 1916, when they were young and hopeful, and all seemed possible. It would not be surprising if his memory were idealised – he had died young, leaving only glorious memories.

However, it seems clear that he did indeed 'do his best' and was an inspirational officer, dealing with an ultimately impossible situation by bringing to bear all the warcraft he had studied for years. Apart from a fundamental commitment to soldiering as a career, other factors drove him to fight; he inherited a need to fulfil the dreams of the father he had never known, and an absolute acceptance of the ideals of his uncle John, no matter how much they disagreed, and of a family whose commitment to the republican cause never wavered.

In 1966, during the commemorations of the fiftieth anniversary of the Easter Rising, railway stations were renamed after the executed leaders. Limerick Station was named after Con Colbert, from Athea, County Limerick. Edward Daly's name was given to the railway station in Bray, County Wicklow, although he had no apparent connection with this area.

In Limerick, there are few traces of one of its more famous sons. Edward Daly is portrayed on the monument on Sarsfield Bridge, over the Shannon; this also commemorates Con Colbert, another executed leader, and Tom Clarke, because of his marriage into a Limerick family. On 15 July 1983, the Mid-Western Health Board offices in Limerick city, at 31-33 Catherine Street, were officially named 'The Comdt. Edward Daly House'. Since then, the health board has been abolished. The building is not now open to the public, and the plaque unveiled at the time is hidden from view. A portrait of Edward Daly was officially unveiled in the Officers' Mess of Sarsfield Barracks, Limerick, on 11 June 1982. A plaque on 15 Barrington Street, erected by the Thomond Archaeological Society, commemorates both John and Edward Daly. It was unveiled by President Éamon de Valera on 22 May 1966. A more individual recognition of Edward Daly in the city which formed him would be a fitting tribute.

1916

... Was it wisdom or glorious folly?
They were of us, our brothers, our own,
They had loved the same land, they were flesh of our flesh,
Bone of our very bone;
Their foemen took them and judged them,
And shot them in secret apart,
Then we heard in the terrible silence
The sob of a nation's heart.[22]

Appendix 1

The Daly Sisters
• • • • • • • •

Descendants of the Daly family still live in Limerick, but the surname of that branch of the Dalys was extinguished with Edward's death. Those of his sisters who married used 'Daly' as a middle name for their children.

Ned's mother, Catharine Daly, died in 1937, and was given a massive funeral in Limerick. The last of Edward Daly's sisters died in 1973.

The shock of the failure of the Rising and Edward's execution, followed rapidly by the death of John Daly, drove the family into mourning and reduced their interest in public activities. Their home was raided more than once by the Black and Tans during the War of Independence, and was again raided during the Civil War, this time by Free State troops, as the family was strongly anti-Treaty.

Eileen Daly, the eldest daughter, married Edward (Ned) O'Toole in 1905. Edward later became city treasurer of Limerick. They had two sons, John Daly (known as Daly) and Éamon. When the sons were in their teens, the family moved to the USA for some years, but later returned to Limerick. Daly became secretary of O'Mara's bacon factory.

Madge Daly, born on 4 Feb 1877, was the businesswoman of the family. John Daly left her everything in his will, including the leasehold of 26 William Street, and she became manager of Daly's Bakery. In October 1916 she received a High Court summons for £11.14.0 outstanding income tax, but she ignored this, and it was never followed up. Madge ultimately owned a number of properties in Limerick, and was a source of financial aid both to her sisters' families and to a new Limerick battalion of the Volunteers. Practical help was also given to Volunteers who had fought in the Rising. Ernest Blythe says, 'There were three Volunteers from Dublin ... working in Limerick, two of them with the Daly family. They had lost their jobs in Dublin and Madge Daly had brought them to Limerick.'[1]

Madge remained in charge of Limerick Cumann na mBan until 1924. She also helped to establish a new Limerick battalion of the IRA after the Easter Rising, the Second Battalion, and gave it a good deal of financial help. Relations between both battalions were poor for many years; the Daly family never really forgave the first Limerick battalion for not having come out during the Rising, and there was great bitterness against the leaders for having surrendered their arms. The Daly sisters, with Ernest Blythe, stigmatised the Limerick Battalion officers, and it was Blythe who established the Second Battalion.

The two battalions never worked well together, but were finally united in March 1921.[2]

The bakery was raided and damaged by Free State troops during the Civil War, but compensation was later paid. Innovative as always, the bakery introduced a motor van to serve deliveries to Ardnacrusha, when the Shannon Electric Scheme was under construction (1924–9).

Widowed by the Easter Rising, Kathleen Daly Clarke was the only member of the family who went into politics, wishing to keep the flame of Tom's ideals alive. A founder member of Fianna Fáil, she was a TD (member of the Irish parliament) and a senator, and in 1939 became the first woman lord mayor of Dublin. Her two elder sons spent much of their childhood in Limerick with their aunts, but she kept the youngest, Emmet, with her as much as possible. She lived for many years in Sandymount, Dublin, first on her own and then with her eldest son Daly and his wife Mary. In her latter years she moved to Liverpool to live with her youngest son Dr Emmet Clarke, his wife Ellen and their two sons. She died on 29 September 1972, and was given a state funeral in Dublin. Her memoir was published in 1991 by O'Brien Press, under the title *Revolutionary Woman*.

Agnes Daly never married. During the War of Independence she was brutalised one evening by a gang of Black and Tans; her hair was cut off, and her hand split with a knife, almost severing her thumb. Carrie, who had trained in first aid, managed to repair the wound temporarily; because of the curfew, a doctor could not be reached that night. The man responsible for the knife attack was sent out of Limerick the following day. A very straight, direct-speaking woman, Agnes worked in the bakery shop for many years, and was the chief housekeeper at home. She had worked as a dressmaker with her sister Kathleen, until the latter moved to America to marry Tom Clarke.

Laura Daly (born 1882) was Ned Daly's dearest sister, and his champion whenever he fought with their uncle John. In fact, after the final row which caused Ned's departure from Limerick in 1913, Laura is said never to have spoken to her uncle again. In 1918, she married Jim O'Sullivan, Ned's closest friend, after his release from internment. Still an IRA organiser, Jim was on the run at the time, living in the Dalys' attic and referred to as 'Mary' when strangers were near. They were married very romantically at midnight in a Limerick chapel, and had two sons and two daughters. Jim managed Daly's bakehouse, and he and Laura later started a restaurant at 3 O'Connell Street, Limerick. Jim stayed out of the Civil War, although his wife's family were actively opposed to the Treaty. He had greatly admired Michael Collins since their internment, and Collins was godfather to his son John. Jim probably opposed the Treaty, but would not oppose Collins.

During the 1930s depression, Jim had a disagreement with Madge and left the bakery. Shortly afterwards he was employed by the Hospitals Trust. Working with the Trust meant that he had to live in Dublin for some years with his sister Mollie, but he was eventually sent back to run a Hospitals Trust office in 3 O'Connell Street, Limerick. He later worked in an administrative capacity in O'Sullivan's Shoes, 114 Upper O'Connell Street, Limerick, established by his son Ned in 1947. O'Sullivan's Shoes opened a specialist children's shoe-shop in what had been the old bakery in William Street, and the business remained one of Limerick's premier shoe merchants until it closed in 2009. Laura died in 1967, and Jim in 1973.

Carrie Daly, born on 18 October 1884, never married. When she was sixteen she spent a year in France as an au pair with a widower, a friend of Seán and Maud Gonne Mac-Bride, who had a daughter the same age. She came back with her hair up (unheard-of for a young single woman), having learned to ride a bicycle, very daring at the time. Carrie sang, played the piano, was expert at many types of craft work, and ran Daly's confectionery and cake shop in Sarsfield Street, where she always dressed the windows. Her ambition was to be a nurse, for which she studied first aid, but her mother apparently would not allow it, because she would have had to go to England to train.

Annie, the next sister, was born in 1886, and is described as a very quiet, ladylike girl. She died in 1908, aged only twenty-one, of typhus.

Nora Daly married Éamonn Dore, or de hÓir, bodyguard of Seán MacDiarmada. They lived in Limerick and had one son and two daughters. Éamonn was involved in running the William Street bakery, which finally closed in 1959. He wrote several articles about John Daly and Edward Daly, and was custodian of some of the items Ned gave his sisters before his execution. Éamonn died in 1972, aged seventy-six, and Nora on 4 November 1977, aged eighty-eight.

From about 1920 the three unmarried sisters, Madge, Agnes and Carrie, lived with their mother in 'Ardeevin', a house on the Ennis Road, Limerick. It was this house that was attacked by the Black and Tans in 1921; the contents were piled on the street and burned, while the girls struggled to get their infirm aunt Lollie down the stairs, fearful that the house would be burned as well. Many personal items relating to Ned were lost during this fire. Lollie had to move in with Eileen O'Toole's family, and their mother, Catharine, moved in with her daughter Laura's family, until the damage could be repaired. Lollie died in 1925.

The girls and their mother often took part in rosary vigils outside Limerick barracks during the Civil War, protesting at executions. On one of these occasions the women protesting were attacked by Free State troops. Mrs Daly's shoulder was injured by a blow from a rifle-butt, and never properly healed thereafter.

Two of Kathleen Clarke's sons, Daly and Tom, lived with

their aunts for some time as adults; they had often been cared for by them as children. Daly, who had spent a couple of years in Florida for his health, opened Limerick's first ever soda-fountain beside Daly's Bakery; Tom trained as a confectioner, and worked in the bakery for some years.

Around 1930, the Daly family moved to a house called 'Tivoli' (now Villiers School) on the North Circular Road, Limerick; they needed the space for a live-in nurse for their elderly mother. A fine house with a three-acre garden (a gardener lived on the grounds), Tivoli was a paradise for all their nephews and nieces. It became difficult to heat during the Second World War (1939–45) because of coal shortages, so they moved to a nearby smaller house called 'Cragfield'. The Dalys were among the first to own a motor-car in Limerick, a German Steyr model, and later owned a convertible Ansaldo, an Italian car.

Before the war they were early pioneers of aeroplane journeys as well, travelling periodically to a German spa for Madge's arthritis treatment. This involved a steamer to Hamburg, and a three-hour flight to Cologne. When Madge, Agnes and Laura took this journey together, in 1930, a local newspaper (according to an undated cutting), proudly stated:

> We have never heard before of three sisters travelling at the one time in an aeroplane ... The trip of these Limerick ladies is an event without precedent in the history of air travel.

In 1937 Edward Daly's mother, Catharine, died, aged eighty-five. Around 1945 the three sisters moved to Dublin, first to Avoca Avenue, Blackrock and then to Kill Lane, Foxrock. Madge was suffering from severe arthritis, and needed to be near her specialist. Agnes had recovered from a breast-cancer operation, but was affected by a heart condition, and spent her final years in bed. They lived in a large modern house, 'Lissadell', with two live-in nurses, a cook and a chauffeur.

When Madge died in early 1969, Agnes and Carrie moved back to Limerick, but Agnes died later that year. As Carrie aged, she moved to live with Kathleen's son Tom and his wife Maureen, and died in their care in 1973.

Appendix 2

Edward Daly Letters

• • • • • • • • • •

Letter 1

[no date]

Dear Laura

I was very glad to get your letter and now having made you a confidante you shall probably have to work over-time at it. I am sorry I never did before but it's not too late, now things have straightened out very much. We are going to be formally engaged at end of March, when this term ends. The next term begins May to end of July which finishes three years. She has been offered a two year extension and has refused it as it means italian opera at Convent [sic] Garden, instead of that, if we can't get married soon after July, she has a notion of taking a part in some musical comedy, which would be easy enough to get. – besides which, as she says, the few months stage experience would be always valuable and would enable her to say whatever happens I can make a living at that.

She asked me if you would write her, she says she wants to tell you things. Well if you will, the address is Miss Molly Keegan, 52 Holland Rd, Kensington, London West. Do write, won't you. You know she saw your photo and likes you a lot and I'm sure you will like her.

By the way, I started hustling here the other day and tackled the boss. He refused a 10% increase and I told him I wouldn't be here longer than the time it took me to get another job. I told him also what I thought of his bringing in an auditor friend of his for half the day, an old man, whom everyone in the place as well as the boss knew, did nothing for half the day, leaving everything for me to do in the other half and got twice my pay for it. Do you know what the boss's reply was, 'I thought all the time that you weren't altogether depending on this job. I met some people from Limerick etc etc' – I could have booted him.

Well, anyhow, I looked around here and there is a job expected to become vacant in a week or so and if it does I am almost certain to get it – It is worth about £100 per annum. Hope it comes off. It is in the same line as M.R. & Co. [May Roberts & Company].

I would like to bring Molly down at Easter for the few days. Do you think it might be done. There's another thing, too I must tell you, she's thoroughly Irish and if the necessity was there and I didn't go it would finish me with her.

I must stop here as I am getting busy.

Good Bye Laura, love to all. Ned.

PS. Do you think I'd better tell Mamma. I think I ought to you know.

Letter 2

12 October 1915

Dear Laura

I got your letter on Sunday I think. Tom Jr had put it away in the Hallstand for me and forgot it until Sunday.

I got Fannin's to send that cushion. Hope its all right. It cost more than if I got it from our London House, but there would probably be delays that way. I enclose Fannins Bill. I can see my weekend fading in the distance for two reasons, time and money. Bye the way, tell Mamma to hang on to that cash for the present, you see some people that I know have told me recently that I am a big fool not to get my voice trained and have advised me to get expert opinion from Vincent O'Brien. I am going to see him some day this week. He is the man that trained McCormack and would not touch a voice unless 'twas good. So I will see what he says. He's pretty stiff in his prices though. I am back with K. [Kathleen] but Sean [MacDiarmada] is not there. No more news at present. Will try get down for dance expected someone Sunday But found later no excursion. Everyone his [here] is in good form.

Good By Best Love to Everyone Ned

Wish some of you could come up soon for weekend. Any chance.

Letter 3

[no date]

Monday

Dear Laura

I was expecting a letter from you for some days. I am leaving M.R. on Sat. I can't give you the main reason here, but it was only partly a question of screw [wages]. I'm jolly glad anyhow – I should have done it long ago. I have one or two things in view but nothing definite yet.

Is there any chance of your running up next week when I would be free.

Everybody here is a.1. No more news. Write soon

Ned

Letter 4

[no date]

Thursday

Dearest Mamma

Just a few lines by K. who is going down.

Things here are very tense, no-one knows what might happen. However theres not much cause for you to worry as if trouble starts I will not be just in the firing line – best of being a boss I suppose. Besides I will be wearing a new garment that will stop most things. I must stop here but I suppose it will be some weeks before I can write again, & now there are many things in my head which I cannot write, but Mamma Dear, I want to tell you how I know and appreciate how good you have always been to me & how good all the others have been.

Give my love to everyone

Good Bye, Mamma. Ned

Appendix 3

'Twas on a Glorious Easter Day

'Twas on a glorious Easter day
In brave old Dublin Town,
They lighted Freedom's fires anew
And braved the despot's frown.

Read out the deathless names again!
We love them every one:
Our hearts shall hold their memory green
Till all the days are done.

Clarke, Connolly, the Brothers Pearse,
MacDermott, loved by all,
And Plunkett and O'Hanrahan–
They come at memory's call.

MacDonagh's laugh rings down the years!
MacBride's undaunted soul,
And Eamonn Ceannt's heroic heart
Make bright for us the Goal.

Ned Daly, Heuston, Colbert true–
The young intrepid three
Who died in manhood's glorious dawn
Their Motherland to free.

And Mallin and the Brothers Kent;
And Rory of the Gael,
Who died for us in London Town,
The pride of Gráinne Mhaol.

Some gave their lives with gun in hand;
Their story proudly tell–
O'Rahilly and fifty more,
Who bravely fighting fell.

'Twas on a glorious Easter day
In brave old Dublin Town,
They lighted Freedom's fires anew
And dared the despot's frown.

They brought their shackled Motherland
To Freedom's open door–
God grant their holy dream comes true
Ere one more year is o'er.

Brian na Banban [Brian O'Higgins][1]

Notes

PROLOGUE

1 Kathleen Clarke, *Revolutionary Woman* (O'Brien Press, 1991), p18.

2 *Munster News*, 13 September 1890.

3 *Limerick Reporter and Tipperary Vindicator*, 16 September 1890.

CHAPTER ONE

1 History of John Daly's Fenian activities from articles written by him in *Irish Freedom*, February 1912 to May 1913.

2 Marriage certificate of Edward Daly and Catharine O'Mara, 18 January 1873, in which the groom's profession is given as 'lath cutter' and his address as Ashbourne Road, Limerick: the bride's father Daniel is described as 'coachman'; birth certificate of Margaret (Madge) Daly, 4 February1877; birth certificate of Caroline (Carrie) Daly, 18 October 1884, in which the family address is given as 14 Wellesley Place, Limerick. Caroline is said to have been named for the Marchioness of Queensberry, who took an interest in non-violent Irish nationalism. She helped many nationalist families in difficulties, and may well have aided the Daly family. Visiting the elder Mrs Daly when Catharine Daly was expecting Carrie, she asked if the child could be named for her if it was a girl.

3 I am very grateful to East Sussex Record Office, Lewes, East Sussex, England, where I examined the archives of St George's Asylum, an institution run by the Sisters of St Augustine. The Resident Medical Officer, Dr Mark Ryan, was a Fenian sympathiser, and employed both the Daly brothers. Staff are mentioned occasionally in the records; John Daly's name is recorded because he witnessed the death of a patient, Martin Francis Mahony, on 1 April 1882. John resigned soon afterwards, and was replaced by Edward, who apparently worked there as 'Edward Hayes' (using his mother's maiden name) from 1882 to 1884. His name is not mentioned in the records available.

4 Meeting of Limerick Harbour Board, 15 September, *Munster News*, 17 September 1890.

5 *Munster News*, 20 September 1890.

6 Clarke, *Revolutionary Woman*, p18.

7 James Daly married Honora McMahon from Sixmilebridge, County Clare, in Sydney, Australia, in 1858, later settling in New Caledonia. Michael's third marriage was to Swiss-born Louise Stauffer (born in 1881), with whom he had at least seven children. The Daly descendants in New Caledonia (French-speaking) have always maintained links with the Limerick family, and have detailed family trees of their Irish connections.

8 Clarke, *Revolutionary Woman*, p20.

9 At the time of his death Jim was living at 31 Henry Street. Cholera is caused by a micro-organism entering through the mouth, usually through infected water or food; it spreads mostly through infected water supplies (see Joseph Robins, *The Miasma: epidemic and panic in nineteenth-century Ireland*, IPA (1995)).

10 Patrick Hayes, Limerick. Newspaper cutting, Album No. 3 (1896), Daly Papers, Glucksman Library, University of Limerick.

11 A history of the Burgess Hill area refers to John Daly as a 'Notorious Dynamitard', and describes him as a 'social favourite in Burgess Hill' while he worked there: AH Gregory, *The Story of Burgess Hill*, Charles Clarke Ltd (1933).

12 RV Comerford, 'The Parnell Era', *A New History of Ireland, Vol. VI, Ireland Under the Union II: 1870–1921*, Oxford University Press (1996), p66.

13 Alderman Manton, of the Birmingham Watch Committee, wrote to the Home Secretary: 'Mr Farndale [Birmingham chief constable] said it was not exactly the police who planted the explosives on Daly, but a companion and confederate of Daly, who was in the employment of the Irish police ... [T]he explosives were procured in America, and delivered to the confederate of Daly ...' (*Munster News*, 24 September 1890).

14 Letter to Earl Spencer, Lord Lieutenant of Ireland, from Sir Edward Jenkinson, quoted in Christy Campbell, *Fenian Fire*, HarperCollins Publishers (2002), p144.

15 He continued: 'Ay, within the dungeon walls his love would cause him in his memory to visit again the place of his childhood, the recollections of his early youth would come back on him with the glorious and poetic inspiration of his early manhood, and his memory would fly back to the spot where lay the bones

of his father. He would visit in imagination the place where his saintly and widowed mother breathed her last words of love for her persecuted son. Let them
send him to a dungeon. That would not destroy his love. They must call in the
surgeon and cut out his very heart; then and only then could they destroy the
love he bore to the land of his fathers, the land that was so dear to him.'

16 Clarke, *Revolutionary Woman*, p15.

17 Louis Le Roux, *Life and Letters of John Daly*, unpublished manuscript, n.d.,
Daly Papers, Glucksman Library, University of Limerick.

18 Telegram, 8 September 1896, ref. 1993.0110, Limerick County Museum.

19 *Limerick Leader*, 21 August 1896.

20 Eileen Daly filled at least six albums with presscuttings, starting with John's
arrest and imprisonment and continuing to the highlights of his American tour.
These albums are now among the Daly Papers, Glucksman Library, University of
Limerick. Maud Gonne, daughter of a British army officer and lifelong political
activist, was introduced to Fenianism by John O'Leary, president of the Supreme
Council of the IRB (1885–1907), who had spent nine years in British jails.
Maud Gonne later became active in land agitation. High-spirited and immensely
attractive, she was for many years the obsessive love-interest of the poet WB Yeats.

21 Clarke, *Revolutionary Woman*, p22.

22 *Limerick Leader*, 23 June 1897.

23 N Cardozo, *Maud Gonne: Lucky Eyes and a High Heart* (Gollancz, (1978), pp146–7.

24 Le Roux, *Life and Letters of John Daly*.

25 Des Ryan, 'Opposition to the Boer War, Limerick, 1899–1902', *The Old Limerick Journal*, No. 40, Winter 2004.

26 The school registers are available online from Limerick City Museum.

27 Anonymous, 'Sketch of Edward Daly', *Limerick Leader*, 26 May 1934.

28 Helen Litton, 'The Famine in Schools', in Tom Hayden (ed), *Irish Hunger, personal reflections on the legacy of the Famine*, Roberts Rinehart (1997), p63.

29 Catharine O'Mara Daly's mother, Miss de Lacy, had been a governess, and
eloped with a steward, William O'Mara, from a large estate in Quin, County
Clare. They separated after some years, but he continued to turn up at his

daughter's home occasionally. The Daly family's mother, Margaret Hayes, came from Fedamore, County Limerick.

30 Clarke, *Revolutionary Woman*, p14.

31 Louis Le Roux, *Tom Clarke and the Irish Freedom Movement*, Talbot Press (1936), pp30–1.

32 Tom Clarke describes his prison experiences in *Glimpses of an Irish Felon's Prison Life*, Maunsel & Roberts (1922).

33 Le Roux, *Tom Clarke and the Irish Freedom Movement*, p9.

34 Letter, Tom Clarke to John Devoy, 19 December 1908, in W O'Brien and D Ryan (eds), *Devoy's Post Bag, 1871–1928*, 2 vols, Dublin (1948, 1953), Vol. II, p374.

CHAPTER TWO

1 Gerard MacAtasney, *Tom Clarke: Life, Liberty, Revolution*, Merrion (2013), pp188,190–1

2 Éamonn Dore, 'Commandant Edward Daly', *Limerick Leader*, 21 June 1922.

3 I am very grateful to Dr Anne Cameron, Archives Assistant at the Andersonian Library, University of Strathclyde, Glasgow, who provided copies of the student register with this information.

4 Minute Book of Limerick Bakers' Society, Limerick City Archives P39/2: 'August 4th 1909. ... Letter from Mr John Daly asking society to allow his nephew to finish his apprenticeship in the shop, he having spent some of his time in Glasgow. Proposed by Pat Maher, seconded by P. O'Halloran, that he get permission provided he displaced no-one. Counter Resolution moved by John O'Rourke, seconded by Jn. Dwyer Sen., That permission be not given.'

5 Efforts to find archives relating to Spaight's Timber Yard were unsuccessful.

6 W O'Brien and D Ryan (eds), *Devoy's Post Bag*, (2 vols), Dublin (1948, 1953), Vol. II, p395.

7 The writer may have been JJ Lynch; presscutting from Album No. 5, Daly Papers, Glucksman Library, University of Limerick.

8 Personal comment to the author which refers to the practice of pigeon-keeping, the implication here being one of betting, low-life contacts.

9 Efforts to find archives relating to May Roberts were unsuccessful.

10 Anonymous, 'Sketch of Edward Daly', *Limerick Leader*, 26 May 1934.

11 Letters in Daly Papers, Glucksman Library, University of Limerick.

12 Gerard McAtasney, *Seán MacDiarmada, The Mind of the Revolution*, Drumlin Publications (2004), p91.

13 Kathleen Clarke, *Revolutionary Woman*, O'Brien Press (1991), p44.

14 James, born on 20 February 1891, was one of nine children of John and Margaret O'Sullivan, both from County Kerry, and in the 1911 Census was living with his family at 14 Rathdown Terrace, North Circular Road, Dublin. His brother Jack was a postman, and two of his sisters joined Cumann na mBan. The works of Charles Dickens were his favourite reading.

15 The Boys' Brigade was founded in Glasgow in 1883. The boys wore uniforms, and were given some military training.

16 Johnny O'Connor, in interview with Proinsias MacAonghusa, Radio Éireann broadcast, 1966. I am very grateful to Mr O'Connor's daughter, Maeve Conlan, who gave me a typescript copy of this interview.

17 Major-General PJ Hally, 'The Easter Rising in Dublin: The Military Aspects', *The Irish Sword*, Vol. VII (1966), Vol. VIII (1967).

18 Letter from 'Dick', 371 North Circular Rd, Phibsboro, Dublin, to Jim O'Sullivan, 4 May 1918 (courtesy of O'Sullivan family, Limerick).

19 Madge Daly, Cumann na mBan, BMH WS0855.

20 Seán McGarry, IRB member, BMH WS0368.

21 Fionán Lynch, captain, F Company, BMH WS0192.

22 Seán Cronin (ed), *The McGarrity Papers*, Anvil Books (1972), pp36–8.

23 O'Brien and Ryan (eds), *Devoy's Post Bag*, Vol. II, p444 (14 May 1914).

24 Dore, 'Commandant Edward Daly'.

25 PJ Stephenson, *Paddy Joe*, private publication (2006), p3.

26 Liam Ó Briain, recollections in *Cuimhní Cinn*, Sairséal agus Dill (1951, reprinted 1974), pp161–2.

27 Dr Brigid Lyons Thornton, Cumann na mBan, in K Griffith and TE O'Grady,

Curious Journey, An Oral History of Ireland's Unfinished Revolution, Hutchinson (1982), p24.

28 Dr Brigid Lyons Thornton, Cumann na mBan, BMH WS0259.

29 Seán Prendergast, captain, C Company, BMH WS0755.

30 Louis Le Roux, *Tom Clarke and the Irish Freedom Movement*, Talbot Press (1936), p142.

31 Dore, 'Commandant Edward Daly'.

32 McAtasney, *Seán MacDiarmada*, p72.

33 GC Duggan, in LA 24, UCD Archives.

34 Patrick Ramsbottom, BMH WS 1046.

35 Liam O'Carroll, lieutenant, A Company, BMH WS0314.

36 Jerry Golden, B Company, orderly to Ned Daly, BMH WS0522.

37 Seán Cody, C Company, BMH WS 1035.

38 Golden, BMH WS0522.

39 Anonymous, 'Sketch of Edward Daly'.

40 Margaret Browne [Mrs Seán McEntee], Cumann na mBan, BMH WS0322

41 Annie Fahy, Cumann na mBan, BMH WS0202.

42 Le Roux, *Tom Clarke*, pp148–9.

43 Ernest Blythe, IRB, BMH WS939.

44 DMP, Colonial Office papers, February 1915, CO904/164, National Archives, Kew.

45 Le Roux, *Tom Clarke*, pp154–5.

46 Anonymous, 'Sketch of Edward Daly'.

47 Feis Ceoil Archives, Scrapbook 8, National Library of Ireland: Manuscripts Section.

48 *Musical Times and Singing-Class Circular*, Vol. 56, 1915.

49 *Evening Telegraph*, 13 May 1912.

50 I am indebted to Linda Clayton, genealogist, who researched Molly Keegan's life for me with great speed and efficiency. The only photograph available was not suitable for reproduction: *Weekly Irish Times*, 21 December 1912, p12.

51 P Béaslaí, Vice Commandant, First Battalion, BMH WS0261.

52 AJ O'Halloran, Limerick Volunteers, BMH WS1700.

53 Patrick Pearse to Madge Daly, 28 May 1915, in Folder 29, Daly Papers, Glucksman Library, University of Limerick.

54 Michael Brennan, Limerick Volunteers, BMH WS1068.

CHAPTER THREE

1 Kathleen Clarke, *Revolutionary Woman*, O'Brien Press (1991), p56.

2 Seán McGarry, IRB, WS0368.

3 Tom Clarke to Madge Daly, 18 July 1915, Daly Papers, Glucksman Library, University of Limerick.

4 Clarke, *Revolutionary Woman*, p56.

5 Louis Le Roux, *Tom Clarke and the Irish Freedom Movement*, Talbot Press (1936), p164.

6 Frank Robbins, Irish Citizen Army, BMH WS0585.

7 Leslie Price (Bean de Barra), Cumann na mBan, BMH WS1754.

8 Éamonn Dore, 'Commandant Edward Daly', *Limerick Leader*, 21 June 1922.

9 Gerard McAtasney, *Seán MacDiarmada: The Mind of the Revolution*, Drumlin Publications (2004), p79.

10 CO 904/23, RIC Reports, National Archives, Kew.

11 Le Roux, *Tom Clarke*, p179.

12 Joe Lee, 'Towards the Easter Rising 1916', *Sunday Tribune*, 30 July 2000.

13 Clarke, *Revolutionary Woman*, pp61–2.

14 Eamon Dore, BMH WS0153.

15 Clarke, *Revolutionary Woman*, p63.

16 Honor O Brolchain, *Joseph Plunkett*, O'Brien Press (2012), pp347–8.

17 RIC Reports in Mulcahy Papers, UCD Archives.

18 Darrell Figgis, 'Recollections of the Irish War', *The World's Work*, April 1923.

19 Feargus (Frank) De Burca, E Company, Fourth Battalion, BMH WS0694.

20 Seán Kennedy, first lieutenant, C Company, BMH WS0842.

21 Peter Reynolds, dispatch rider, BMH WS0350.

22 Piaras Béaslaí, vice commandant, First Battalion, BMH WS0261.

23 Michael O'Flanagan, section commander, C Company, BMH WS0800.

24 14 March 1916, CO 904/23, RIC Reports, National Archives, Kew.

25 16 March 1916, CO 904/23, DMP Reports, National Archives, Kew.

26 Seán Cody, C Company, BMH WS1035.

27 Jerry Golden, B Company, orderly to Ned Daly, BMH WS0522.

28 Denis McCullough, BMH WS0915.

29 Desmond Ryan, *The Rising: the complete story of Easter Week*, Golden Eagle Books (1957 ed.), p76.

30 Clarke, *Revolutionary Woman*, p71.

31 Gregory Murphy, BMH WS0150.

32 Clarke, *Revolutionary Woman*, p71.

33 Thomas Dowling, C Company, BMH WS0533.

34 Séamus O'Sullivan, captain, B Company, BMH WS0393.

35 Clarke, *Revolutionary Woman*, pp70, 73.

36 Piaras Béaslaí, 'Moods and Memories', *Irish Independent*, February 1964.

37 Private letter to Jim O'Sullivan, 11 April 1935 (courtesy of O'Sullivan family, Limerick).

38 Seán Price, B Company, BMH WS0769.

39 Nicholas Laffan, captain, G Company, BMH WS0201.

40 Letter, Fionán Lynch to Éamonn Dore, 3 December1965, P150/500, UCD Archives.

41 Maurice Collins, F Company, BMH WS0150.

42 O'Flanagan, BMH WS0800.

43 Patrick Kelly, first lieutenant, G Company, BMH WS0781.

44 Michael Staines, BMH WS0284.

45 Eamon Morkan, second lieutenant, A Company; quartermaster, First Battalion, BMH WS0411.

46 Phyllis Morkan, Cumann na mBan, BMH WS0210.

47 Béaslaí, 'Moods and Memories'.

48 Ryan, *The Rising*, p99.

CHAPTER FOUR

1 Desmond Ryan, *The Rising, The complete story of Easter Week*, Golden Eagle Books Limited (1957 ed.), pp203—4.

2 Éamon Duggan, typescript of talk, 'Four Courts Area, Easter 1916', no date (courtesy of O'Sullivan family, Limerick).

3 Peter Reynolds, dispatch rider, BMH WS0350.

4 Peader McNulty, 'History of A Company, 1st Battalion', LA9, UCD Archives.

5 Seán Prendergast, C Company, BMH WS0755.

6 Seán O'Duffy, A Company, BMH WS0313.

7 Reynolds, BMH WS0350.

8 Phyllis Morkan, Cumann na mBan, BMH WS0210.

9 Charles Townshend, *Easter 1916: The Irish Rebellion*, Allen Lane (2005), p204.

10 I am indebted to Dr Terence O'Neill (Colonel of the Irish Army, retired), who gave me invaluable advice on military strategy.

11 Honor O Brolchain, *16 Lives: Joseph Plunkett*, O'Brien Press (2012), pp354—5.

12 FA McKenzie, *The Irish Rebellion*, C Arthur Pearson, London (1916), p55.

13 Paddy Holahan, 'The Four Courts Area', *Capuchin Annual*, 1942, pp231—7.

14 Interview by John Caulhan, broadcast on WNAC Radio, Boston, in 1966. Tom Sheerin, John O'Connor and Frank Shouldice, all of the First Battalion, were interviewed together. I am indebted to John O'Connor's daughter, Mrs Maeve Conlan, who gave me a typescript copy of this interview.

15 Seán Kennedy, 1st Lieutenant, B Company, BMH WS0842.

16 Liam Archer, F Company, BMH WS0819.

17 Liam Archer, 1 October 1964, Mulcahy Papers, UCD Archives.

18 John O'Connor interview with Proinsias Mac Aonghusa, RTÉ broadcast, 1966. I am indebted to Maeve Conlan for a typescript copy of this interview.

19 Leslie Price, Cumann na mBan, BMH WS0769.

20 Éamon Morkan, 2nd Lieutenant, A Company, quartermaster of First Battalion, BMH WS0411.

21 Michael T Foy and Brian Barton, *The Easter Rising*, The History Press (2011), p156.

22 Patrick Kelly, 1st Lieutenant G Company, BMH WS078.

23 Nicholas Laffan, Captain, G Company, BMH WS0201.

24 John F Shouldice, 1st Lieutenant, F Company, BMH WS0162.

25 Gearóid Ua hUallacháin, Fianna Éireann, BMH WS0328.

26 Jerry Golden, B Company, orderly to Ned Daly, BMH WS0521.

27 Séamus O'Sullivan, captain, B Company, BMH WS0393.

28 O'Sullivan, Ibid.

29 Piaras Béaslaí, vice commandant, First Battalion, BMH WS0261.

30 Padraig Yeates, *Lockout: Dublin 1913*, Gill and Macmillan (2000), p109.

31 Personal comment from Mary Monks (who was at school with the author). It should be noted that the name is Monks, and not Monk, as it appears in many sources.

32 P67/8, UCD Archives.

33 Leslie Price, in D Ó Dulaing, *Voices of Ireland*, O'Brien Press (1984), pp96–7. In her witness statement, Price says that it may have been Michael Staines or Gearóid O'Sullivan who gave them the canes (BMH WS0769).

34 Joseph Reynolds, Fianna Éireann, BMH WS0191.

35 Ignatius Callender, section leader, D Company, BMH WS0923.

36 Patrick Kelly, BMH WS078.

37 Joseph McDonough, C Company, BMH WS1082.

38 Eileen Murphy, Cumann na mBan, BMH WS0480.

39 Eilís Ní Riain, Cumann na mBan, BMH WS0568.

40 Paul O'Brien, *Crossfire: The Battle of the Four Courts*, New Island (2012), p45.

41 Laffan, BMH WS0201.

42 Major-General PJ Hally, 'The Easter Rising in Dublin, the Military Aspects', *Irish Sword*, Vol VII (1966), Vol VIII (1967).

43 Julia Grenan, in Ruth Taillon, *Women of 1916*, Beyond the Pale Publications (1996), p71.

44 Callender, BMH WS0923.

45 Jeremiah Cronin, BMH WS1423.

46 Éamonn Dore, BMH WS0153 and WS0392.

47 Alphonsus O'Halloran, BMH WS0910.

48 Seán McGarry, IRB, BMH WS0356.

49 Kathleen Clarke, *Revolutionary Woman*, O'Brien Press (1991), pp79–81.

CHAPTER FIVE

1 Seán Prendergast, captain, C Company, BMH WS0755.

2 Michael O'Flanagan, section leader, C Company, BMH WS0800.

3 Seán Kennedy, lieutenant, C Company, BMH WS0842.

4 George O'Flanagan, C Company, BMH WS0962.

5 Joseph McDonough, C Company, BMH WS1082.

6 Ignatius Callender, section leader, D Company, BMH WS0923.

7 Charles Townshend, *Easter 1916:The Irish Rebellion*, Allen Lane (2005), pp206–7.

8 Louis Le Roux, *Tom Clarke and the Irish Freedom Movement*, Talbot Press Ltd (1936), p223.

9 Brian O'Higgins, *The Soldier's Story of Easter Week*, O'Higgins, Glasnevin, Dublin (1925), p. 42.

10 *Sinn Féin Leaders of 1916*, Cahill and Co., Mulcahy Papers, UCD Archives.

11 National Archives, Kew, London, WO P150/512.

12 Interview by John Caulhan, WNAC Radio, Boston, 1966.

13 Lorcan Collins, *16 Lives: James Connolly*, O'Brien Press (2012), p288.

14 Annie Fahy, Cumann na mBan, BMH WS0202.

15 Nicholas Laffan, captain, G Company, BMH WS0201.

16 O'Higgins, *The Soldier's Story*, p42; *Pictorial Review of 1916*, Parkside Press (1946), p37.

17 Lord Dunsany, *Patches of Sunlight*, Baltimore (1938), pp283–4.

18 Patrick Holahan, 'The Four Courts Area', *Capuchin Annual*, 1942, pp231–7.

19 John O'Connor, interview with Proinsias Mac Aonghusa, RTÉ broadcast, 1966.

20 Holahan, 'The Four Courts Area'.

21 EJ Duggan, 'Four Courts Area Easter 1916', undated typescript (courtesy of O'Sullivan family, Limerick).

22 Sir John Maxwell, *Daily Mail*, May 1916.

23 National Archives, Kew, London, WO 35/67/3.

24 *Irish Times Sinn Féin Rebellion Handbook*, *Irish Times* (1916), pp210–11.

25 Max Caulfield, *The Easter Rebellion*, Gill and Macmillan (1995), pp292–3.

26 Desmond Ryan, *The Rising*, Golden Eagle Books Ltd (1949), pp215–16; Roger McHugh (ed), *Dublin 1916*, p239.

27 McHugh, *Dublin 1916*, pp233–5.

28 Fearghal McGarry, *The Rising: Ireland: Easter 1916*, Oxford University Press (2010), p187.

29 National Archives, Kew, London, WO 70/6639, Kitchener to Maxwell, 23 May 1916.

30 Caulfield, *The Easter Rebellion*, p294.

31 John F Shouldice, first lieutenant, F Company, BMH WS0162.

32 Holahan, 'The Four Courts Area'.

33 Patrick Kelly, first lieutenant, G Company, BMH WS0781.

34 Éamonn Dore, 'Commandant Edward Daly', *Limerick Leader*, 21 June 1922.

35 'In Memory of Elizabeth O'Farrell', National Commemoration Committee, The Workers' Party (1981), pp6-7.

36 FA McKenzie, *The Irish Rebellion – What Happened and Why*, C Arthur Pearson, London (1916), p87.

37 Unpublished statement by Sister Agnes, 17 May 1966. I am very grateful to my cousin Michael O'Nolan, of Limerick, for providing a copy of this statement.

38 Piaras Béaslaí, *Irish Independent*, 20 January 1953.

39 Brigid Lyons Thornton, in K Griffith and TE O'Grady, *Curious Journey*, Hutchinson (1982), pp76–8.

40 Michael T Foy and Brian Barton, *The Easter Rising*, The History Press (2011 ed.), pp167–8.

41 Lyons Thornton, in *Curious Journey*, pp74–5.

42 Éamon Morkan, second lieutenant, A Company, BMH WS0411.

43 O'Connor, MacAonghusa interview.

44 O'Connor, Ibid.

45 Liam Hogan, letter to the author, 31 March 1986.

46 Seán Price, B Company, BMH WS0769.

47 Seán McLoughlin, Fianna, BMH WS0290.

48 Sheerin, WNAC Radio Boston interview, 1966.

49 Joseph O'Rourke, IRB, BMH WS1244.

50 Dore, 'Commandant Edward Daly'; Le Roux, *Tom Clarke*, pp229–30; Éamonn Dore, BMH WS0153.

51 Major-General PJ Hally, 'The Easter Rising in Dublin, The Military Aspects', *The Irish Sword*, Vol. VII (1966), Vol. VIII (1967).

CHAPTER 6

1 Patrick Kelly, BMH WS0781.

2 Brian O'Higgins, *Wolfe Tone Annual*, 1935.

3 Liam Ó Briain, *Cuimhní Cinn*, Sairséal agus Dill (1951, reprinted 1974). I am indebted to Deirdre Shortall for her translation of the Irish text. Ó Briain names the song as 'When a man's in love', but this is a Scottish folksong, not one from the Gilbert and Sullivan light operas. However, Daly may well have sung several songs from his repertoire.

4 Leon Ó Broin, *W E Wylie and the Irish Revolution*, Gill and Macmillan (1989), p36.

5 John Dillon to John Redmond, 30 April 1916, quoted in Robert McKee, *The Green Flag*, Weidenfeld & Nicolson (1972), p573.

6 Michael T Foy and Brian Barton, *The Easter Rising*, The History Press (2011 edition), pp294–6.

7 Foy and Barton, Ibid, p305.

8 Michael Soughley, DMP, BMH WS0189.

9 Lord Dunsany, *Patches of Sunlight*, Baltimore (1938), p274.

10 National Archives, Kew, London, W/O 79/6639, Maxwell to Kitchener, 11 May 1916; de Valera Papers, P150/512, UCD Archives.

11 Madge Daly memoir, in Piaras Mac Lochlainn, *Last Words*, Kilmainham Gaol Restoration Society (1971), p72. The original is kept with the Daly Papers, Glucksman Library, University of Limerick.

12 Mac Lochlainn, *Last Words*, p73.

13 I am deeply grateful to Siobhán de hÓir, the widow of Éamonn de hÓir, who discovered the items in her home, and enabled me to examine and photograph them.

14 Mac Lochlainn, *Last Words*, p72.

15 Benedict Cullen,'Echoes of the Rising's final shots', *Irish Times*, 19 April 2003, p3.

16 Margaret O'Callaghan, Cumann na mBan, BMH WS0747.

17 Anonymous priest (probably Fr Albert or Fr Sebastian), *Catholic Bulletin*, July 1916; quoted by Brian O'Higgins, *Wolfe Tone Annual*, 1946.

18 National Archives, Kew, London, WO 35/67/2: Executions.

19 National Archives, Kew, London, WO 71/344.

20 Ibid.

21 Brian Hughes, *16 Lives: Michael Mallin*, O'Brien Press (2012), p200.

22 Anonymous, in de Valera Papers, P150/470, UCD Archives.

APPENDIX 1

1 Ernest Blythe, *Gaeil á Múscailt (Chuimhní Cinn III)*, Sairséal agus Dill (1973), p123. I am indebted to Deirdre Shortall for the English translation.

2 John O'Callaghan, 'The Limerick Volunteers and 1916', in Ruán O'Donnell (ed), *The Impact of the 1916 Rising Among the Nations*, Irish Academic Press (2008), pp17–18.

APPENDIX 3

1 *Wolfe Tone Annual,* Special 1916 Number, 1935, Publisher Brian O'Higgins, 68 Upr O'Connell Street, Dublin.

Bibliography

ORIGINAL SOURCES

De Valera Papers, UCD Archives

Feis Ceoil Archives, National Library of Ireland

Limerick City Archives

Mulcahy Papers, UCD Archives

War Office Papers, National Archives, Kew, London

Royal College of Music, London

Andersonian Library, University of Strathclyde, Glasgow

PRINTED PUBLICATIONS

Anonymous ['Carol'], 'Sketch of Edward Daly', *Limerick Leader* (26 May 1934).

Barton, Brian, *The Secret Court Martial Records of the Easter Rising*, The History Press (2010 edition).

Béaslaí, Piaras, 'Moods and Memories,' *Irish Independent* (February, 1964).

Campbell, Christy, *Fenian Fire*, HarperCollins*Publishers* (2002).

Cardozo, Nancy, *Maud Gonne: Lucky Eyes and a High Heart*, Gollancz (1978).

Caulfield, Max, *The Easter Rebellion*, Gill and Macmillan (1963, new edition 1995).

Clarke, Kathleen, *Revolutionary Woman: Kathleen Clarke 1878–1972* (ed Helen Litton), O'Brien Press (1991, new edition 2008).

Clarke, Thomas, *Glimpses of an Irish Felon's Prison Life*, Maunsel & Roberts (1922).

Collins, Lorcan, *16 Lives: James Connolly*, O'Brien Press (2012).

Comerford, RV, 'The Parnell Era' in *A New History of Ireland, Vol VI, Ireland under the Union II: 1870–1921*, Oxford University Press (1996).

Connell, Joseph EA jnr, *Dublin in Rebellion, a Directory 1913–1923*, Lilliput Press (2009 edition).

Cronin, Sean (ed), *The McGarrity Papers*, Anvil Books (1972).

Cullen, Benedict, 'Echoes of the Rising's final shots,' *Irish Times* (19 April, 2003).

Daly, John, 'Memoirs of a Fenian,' *Irish Freedom* (February 1912–May 1913).

Daly, Madge, 'Gallant Cumann na mBan of Limerick', in JM MacCarthy (ed), *Limerick's Fighting Story*, Anvil Books (1966), pp85–92.

de hÓir, Nóra, *Laochra Luimnigh: Uí Dhálaigh Luimnigh agus Éirí Amach na Cásca 1916*, Cló Saoirse – Irish Freedom Press (2001).

de hÓir, Nóra, 'Seán Ó Dálaigh – duine a mhair ar son na hÉireann', *North Munster Antiquarian Journal*, Vol XXI (1979), pp39–49

Dore, Éamonn, 'Limerick Patriot: Commandant Edward Daly,' *Limerick Leader* (21 June 1922).

Dunsany, Lord, *Patches of Sunlight*, Baltimore (1938).

Figgis, Darrell, 'Recollections of the Irish War,' *The World's Work* (April, 1923).

Foy, Michael T and Barton, Brian, *The Easter Rising*, The History Press (2011 edition).

Gregory, AH, *The Story of Burgess Hill*, Charles Clarke Ltd (1933).

Griffith, Kenneth and O'Grady, Timothy E, *Curious Journey, an oral history of Ireland's unfinished revolution*, Hutchinson (1982).

Hally, Major-General PJ, 'The Easter Rising in Dublin, The Military Aspects,' *The Irish Sword*, Vol VII (1966), Vol VIII (1967); reprinted in Harman Murtagh (ed), *Irishmen in War 1800–2000, Essays from* The Irish Sword, Irish Academic Press (2006), Vol II pp97–121.

Holahan, Patrick, 'The Four Courts Area,' *Capuchin Annual* (1942), pp231–7.

Hughes, Brian, *16 Lives: Michael Mallin*, O'Brien Press (2012).

'In Memory of Elizabeth O'Farrell,' National Commemoration Committee, The Workers' Party (1981).

Irish Times Sinn Féin Rebellion Handbook, Irish Times (1916).

Kee, Robert, *The Green Flag*, Weidenfeld and Nicolson (1972).

Lee, Joseph, 'Ireland in the 20th Century', articles on Easter Rising, *Sunday Tribune* (July-August, 2000).

Le Roux, Louis, 'Life and Letters of John Daly', unpublished manuscript (n.d.), Daly Papers, Glucksman Library, University of Limerick.

Le Roux, Louis, *Tom Clarke and the Irish Freedom Movement*, Talbot Press (1936).

Litton, Helen, 'The Famine in Schools,' in Tom Hayden (ed), *Irish Hunger, personal reflections on the legacy of the Famine*, Roberts Rinehart (1997).

MacAtasney, Gerard, *Seán MacDiarmada, The Mind of the Revolution*, Drumlin

Publications (2004).

MacAtasney, Gerard, *Tom Clarke: Life, Liberty, Revolution*, Merrion (2013).

MacCarthy, JM (ed), *Limerick's Fighting Story*, Anvil Books (1966).

McGarry, Fearghal, *The Rising, Ireland: Easter 1916*, Oxford University Press (2010).

McHugh, Roger (ed), *Dublin 1916*, Arlington Books (1966).

McKenzie, FA, *The Irish Rebellion*, C Arthur Pearson, London (1916).

Mac Lochlainn, Piaras F, *Last Words*, Kilmainham Jail Restoration Society (1971).

McNulty, Peader, 'History of A Company, 1st Battalion', LA9, UCD Archives.

Madden, Captain M, 'Address on Presentation of portrait of Commdt. Edward Daly, Limerick', 11 June 1982 (in private hands).

O'Brien, Paul, *Crossfire, The Battle of the Four Courts, 1916*, New Island (2012).

O'Brien, William and Ryan, Desmond (eds), *Devoy's Post Bag 1871–1928* (2 vols), CJ Fallon Ltd (1948, 1953).

Ó Briain, Liam, *Chuimhní Cinn*, Sairséal agus Dill (1951, reprinted 1974).

O Brolchain, Honor, *16 Lives: Joseph Plunkett*, O'Brien Press (2012).

Ó Dulaing, Donncha, *Voices of Ireland*, O'Brien Press (1984).

Ó Gríofa, Ciarán, 'John Daly – The Fenian Mayor' in David Lee (ed), *Remembering Limerick*, Limerick Civic Trust (1997), pp197–203.

O'Higgins, Brian, *The Soldier's Story of Easter Week*, Brian Ó hUiginn (1925).

Robins, Joseph, *The Miasma: epidemic and panic in nineteenth-century Ireland*, Institute of Public Administration (1995).

Ryan, Des, 'Opposition to the Boer War, Limerick, 1899–1902,' *The Old Limerick Journal*, No. 40 (Winter 2004).

Ryan, Desmond, *The Rising: The Complete Story of Easter Week*, Golden Eagle Books Limited (1949).

Sinn Féin Leaders of 1916, Cahill and Co, Mulcahy Papers, UCD Archives.

Stephenson, Patrick Joseph, *Paddy Joe 1895–1960*, published by Jim Stephenson, 111 Manchester Road, Sheffield S10 5DH (2006).

Taillon, Ruth, *Women of 1916*, Beyond the Pale Publications (1996).

Townshend, Charles, *Easter 1916, The Irish Rebellion*, Allen Lane (2005).

Yeates, Padraig, *Lockout: Dublin 1913*, Gill and Macmillan (2000).

Index

McCartan, Pat, 45
McCartney, Mr, 149
McCormack, Captain, 58
McCormack, John, 41, 76
McCullough, Denis, 45, 86
MacCurtain, Tomás, 68, 131–2
MacDiarmada, Seán, 45–6, 47,
  56, 60, 77, 86, 94, 130
  Connolly disappearance,
  79–80
  execution, 181, 183
  in GPO, 122, 129, 131–2
  and Hobson, 93
  in Limerick, 51, 68
  and MacNeill, 91–2, 96,
  98–9
MacDonagh, Thomas, 72, 91,
  167, 172
McDonough, Joseph, 124, 136,
  155, 160
MacEntee, Seán, 103
McEvoy, Christy, 121
McGarrity, Joe, 51–2
McGarry, Milo, 131
McGarry, Seán, 50–1
McGuinness, Joe, 93, 160
McLoughlin, Seán, 162
MacMahon, Phil, 92
MacNeill, Eoin, 47, 78, 81, 86,
  88, 93–4
  countermand, 95–9, 102,
  129–30
  opposed to Rising, 91–2
MacSwiney, Mary, 132
MacSwiney, Terence, 68, 131–2
Magazine Fort, Phoenix Park,
  106–7
Mallin, Michael, 171, 184
Markievicz, Countess
  Constance, 44, 96, 169
Mary's Lane, 107, 109
Maxwell, General Sir John,
  138, 169–70
  on Daly, 174–5
  North King Street violence,
  145, 148, 150–1
May Roberts Wholesale
  Chemists, 43, 60, 75–6
Medical Mission, Charles
  Street, 114, 136–7
Mendicity Institute, 104, 106
Mid-Western Health Board,
  185
Military Council, IRB, 68,
  86–7
  and Connolly, 78–80

date of Rising, 80, 87–8
  and Hobson, 93–4
  Proclamation signed, 87
Monks's Bakery, 120, 150
Monteith, Robert, 60–1, 82
Moore Street, 83–4, 118,
  162, 163
Moore's coach-works, 119,
  140, 153, 154
Morkan, Éamon, 94, 97–8, 102,
  105, 139, 141
  surrender, 159, 163–4
Morkan, Edward Daly, 98
Morkan, Phyllis, 97, 98, 103,
  112, 128, 135–6
Mount Street Bridge, 124, 150
Mountjoy Square, 111–12
Munster News, 14–15, 18,
  19–20, 20–1
Murnane family, 123
Murphy, Fr Columbus, 180
Murphy, Eileen, 125
Murphy, Gregory, 88

Nathan, Sir Matthew, 169
National Museum of Ireland,
  157, 178–9
National Volunteers, 57
New Caledonia, 21–2
Ní Riain, Eilís, 125
Noonan, Michael, 149
North Brunswick Street, 107,
  110, 113, 119–20, 125, 153,
  156, 181
  surrender, 165
North Circular Road, 96,
  115–18
North Dublin Union (NDU),
  104, 105, 107, 113, 126, 150
  Daly's gun, 156–7
North King Street, 134, 137,
  166
  army advances, 124, 144–5,
  153
  barricades, 107–10, 143–5
  civilian casualties, 145–51
  Lancer shot, 113–14
  population, 119
  surrender, 165
North Midlands Division,
  59th, 115
North Staffordshire regiment,
  154
Northumberland Road, 124

Ó Briain, Liam, 53–4, 168

O'Brien, Vincent, 41, 76
O'Brien Press, 189
O'Callaghan, Denis, 119,
  180–1
O'Callaghan, Father, 155
O'Carroll, Liam, 58, 135
O'Connell, Daniel, 17
O'Connell Street, 105, 115,
  139
  surrender, 161–2
O'Connor, Johnny, 48–9, 108,
  111, 138–9, 142–3
  surrender, 159–61
O'Connor, Séamus, 79
O'Donovan Rossa, Jeremiah,
  70, 71–2
  funeral, 72–5
O'Duffy, Seán, 102
O'Farrell, Elizabeth, 155
O'Flanagan, George, 136
O'Flanagan, Michael, 83–4, 90,
  94–5, 103, 134–5, 152
O'Flanagan, Patrick, 152
O'Halloran, Alphonsus, 130
O'Hanrahan, Michael, 171,
  180, 182
O'Hegarty, Lt, 109
O'Higgins, Brian, 100, 168
Old Bailey, London, 35–6
O'Mara, Catharine. see Daly,
  Mrs Catharine
O'Mara's bacon factory, 188
O'Rahilly, The, 118, 129
O'Reilly, Mrs, 146
O'Sullivan, Dolly, 112
O'Sullivan, Edward Daly, 191
O'Sullivan, Gearóid, 51
O'Sullivan, James (Jim), 64,
  112, 125, 190–1
  arrest, 165
  bridge destruction, 115–18
  and Daly, 47–8, 49, 53–4, 60,
  65, 73, 77
  and Rising, 78, 89–90, 92,
  94, 98, 102
    MacNeill countermand,
    95–6, 97
  surrender, 162–3
O'Sullivan, John Daly, 190
O'Sullivan, Mary, 179
O'Sullivan, Mollie, 112, 191
O'Sullivan's Shoes, 191
O'Toole, Éamon, 187–8
O'Toole, Edward (Ned), 37,
  187–8
O'Toole, Eileen. *see* Daly, Eileen